O UGHTEN
H OUSE
P UBLICATIONS

"Ascension Books for the Rising Planetary Consciousness"

Invocation to Light

I live within the Light.
I love within the Light.
I laugh within the Light.
I AM sustained and nourished by the Light.
I joyously serve the Light.
For I AM the Light.
I AM the Light. I AM the Light. I AM. I AM. I AM.

— Archangel Ariel,
Channeled by Tachi-ren

An Ascension Handbook

MATERIAL CHANNELED FROM SERAPIS

by

Tony Stubbs

Editing & Typography by Sara Benjamin-Rhodes
Cover Illustration by Gaia Gent-Wolf
Published by Oughten House Publications
Livermore, California, USA

An Ascension Handbook

MATERIAL CHANNELED FROM SERAPIS

Cover Illustration by Gaia Gent-Wolf
Editing & Typography by Sara Benjamin-Rhodes

Published by

Oughten House Publications

P.O. Box 2008
Livermore, California, 94551-2008 USA

Library of Congress Cataloging-in-Publication Data
Serapis (Spirit)
    An ascension handbook : channeled material from Serapis/ by Tony Stubbs : cover & illustrations by Gaia Gent-Wolf
    p.   cm.
    ISBN 1-880666-08-1 (alk. paper): $11.95
    1. Spirit writings.   2. Ascension of the soul — Miscellanea.
    3. Vibration — Miscellanea. I. Stubbs, Tony, 1947-   . II. Title.
    BF1301.S37   1992
    133.9' 3 — dc20   92-35242
                                                     CIP

ISBN 1-880666-08-1, Quality Trade Publication

Printed in the United States of America
Printed on recycled paper

Contents

{*continued*}

Acknowledgments

For many years now, I have been closely associated with Tachi-ren and Angelic Outreach. I was there the first night Tachi channeled Orin, an aspect of Archangel Ariel, and have attended just about every occasion that Tachi has channeled Ariel since then. I would like to use this opportunity to acknowledge the support of Tachi's love, vision, and inspiration. For several years, Ariel has been bringing new energy techniques onto the planet through Tachi, so it was no surprise when Serapis referred to several of these techniques and suggested that we use them in this book. The flood of upper-dimensional information and techniques just keeps building, as our planet and her inhabitants increase their vibratory frequency at an ever increasing rate. If you are interested in any of the techniques in this book, or in the new information that Tachi-ren is bringing in on Light technologies, please contact the publisher.

I am also deeply indebted to Sara Benjamin for her fine work as the editor of this book.

Publisher's Note

The channeled material in this book is presented essentially as it was received. The reader's interpretation of this or any other channeled information is subject to his or her ego and belief systems.

The language used in this book has been chosen to reflect the actual transmission from the Ascended Master, Serapis, with the least alteration in meaning. Consequently, there may be a few words presented which are not commonly used. Minor editorial enhancements have been made in this edition, to facilitate the flow and reader's comprehension of the material. However, the essence of the channeled material remains unchanged.

Gracious appreciation is given to the Literary Producers of Oughten House for making this publication possible: Marge and John Melanson, Barbara Rawles, Robin Drew, Irit Levy, Debbie Detwiler, Kiyo Monro, Alice Tang, Eugene P. Tang, Brad Clarke, Kathy Cook, Victor R. Beasley, Ph.D., Fred J. Tremblay, Nicole Christine, Dennis Donahue, Kimberly K. Mullen, and Ruth Dutra. Special thanks to the fine staff of Oughten House whose hard work and enthusiasm kept things rolling despite insurmountable pressures: Kim Crawford, Trish Calcote, Robin Rubero, Ariane An-Rah, and Anita Jarrett-Gerard.

⌒ Preface ⌒

The first draft of this book was written over a three week period in January, 1989. In December 1988, I had become aware of an energy about me which announced itself as Serapis and said that its function was to foster the intellectual clarity and discipline required for ascension.

I began an internal dialogue with Serapis and, in early January, Serapis announced the intention to write a book with me on the subject of ascension. We quickly established a writing pattern. I would begin each session by inviting Serapis in and just begin to write. Often, I would sense Serapis probing my memory for a concept or phrase but, having put an idea into my head, Serapis left the expression part up to me.

Although I didn't realize it at the time, I now know my energy is that of Serapis, and we are sufficiently close in frequency that the flow of thought is "seamless": we merge consciousness. The result is a combination of new material from Serapis and what I already knew consciously, selected and arranged by Serapis. As I began to use the techniques that this book offers, the connection became stronger.

So, early in January, 1989, I came to know firsthand the reality of the non-physical world as the source of everything. Following this intense inner paradigm shift, Serapis began this book. The manuscript then sat on a shelf until August,1991, when Serapis once again prodded me to get the word out. Much had happened in the intervening two-and-a-half years, both personally and planetarily, and Serapis and I took this opportunity to bring the manuscript up to date. In October,1991, the planet and her population went through a tremendous shift and again the book went on hold until March,1992. Many of the rules of the game changed in that period, and it now feels to me as though Lightworkers need to be more grounded and earthy. Also, the emphasis seems to have shifted to co-creation through group work. In this new reality, we seem less bent on "personal ascension or bust," and more on "together we can do it."

Over the years, the Serapis material has really brought home to me, at the conscious level, that the realm of Spirit is not something apart from us. It is us, a higher-frequency part of us, and moving up to this frequency is as easy as we believe it to be. We are not separate. Spirit is not something we have. It is what we are, or as some folks say, we are something that Spirit has. I hope this book brings it home that we are not humans having a spiritual experience, but Spirit having a human experience. We are part of a much larger entity, just like an employee of a company is a part of that company, one with a specific and unique function and perspective.

After many years, I've come to know at a deep inner level that I am not something separate and apart from Spirit, that we form a continuum of being in which only the perspective differs, and that a perspective experienced from "within" a physical body allows unique perceptions and ways of being.

For me, this realization was a multi-step process. Through contact with numerous channeled entities over the years, I had picked up an intellectual appreciation of the non-physical universe around us. But it took a series of events (not always pleasant) to awaken me emotionally and begin to release what was stored at the cellular level of my physical body. As we'll see, this is necessary because, in order to ascend with the physical body, we must increase its frequency to that of the Lightbody. Some of us choose to do this slowly over time, and others choose a faster, more turbulent route. Whatever your path, know that you are guided and protected at each step.

This book invites you to review how you see the relationship between the physical, emotional, mental, and Spirit. As you read, do so first with an open heart chakra. Sense the energy behind and within the words. Let your spirit and Serapis flesh out your understanding as you read. Later you can go back and analyze the material from an intellectual perspective. Let understanding filter in during your first reading without mental judgement. The book is short enough to allow more than one reading. It's also somewhat non-linear, because Serapis may approach the same concept from a number of different directions.

Only a handful of people have been in space and seen planet Earth in her entirety. The rest of us may have difficulty in visualizing the planet hanging in space, and may use a model to assist — the familiar globe. Now, of course, no-one would mistake the model for the real thing in this case. Similarly, when it comes to metaphysics in general and ascension in particular, the truth is so vast and incomprehensible that it would be a mistake to think that we could grasp it from where we stand. So, we are given models that we can grasp to open our understanding a little at a time. This book is one such model, a tiny flicker in the dark that together with other flickers will light our path.

I am reminded of the first time I saw the Grand Canyon. I had read the statistics, studied maps, and seen photos, but nothing could have prepared me for the real thing, and I just stood in stunned silence and gratitude for such beauty on our planet. I have a sneaking feeling that ascension may prove to be very similar.

Please enjoy this book. The message is powerful, but it's also light and fun. So, step into the Light and have fun.

Tony Stubbs
Denver, Colorado

✺ Introduction ✺

My name is Serapis. It is usually associated with ancient mystery schools, but my energy is much older than that. I was worshipped as the god Osiris in Atlantis, as Hermes Trimegestus and Thoth, and have been active on this planet for far longer than that.

Obviously, the activities of the mystery schools were not disclosed, and that has led to legends about the teachings and initiation rites. These rites were deliberately taxing in order to generate public awe and respect for initiates, but the main reason for such vigorous testing was to change the self-image of new initiates. They believed that passing the tests marked them out as having special psychic abilities and knowledge. This belief, of course, made the acquisition of such knowledge and abilities much easier. Most initiates didn't realize that everyone had these abilities and that only ignorance kept them dormant. All could ascend but only the initiated believed that they could.

That brings us to you. You may not see yourself as an initiate in a modern day mystery school, but you are. Most of what the initiates of old were taught is generally available in books, including this one. Also, the same types of instruction in psychic abilities are readily available today. If this surprises you, remember that most of the population in earlier days was illiterate and ruled by what you would call primitive superstition.

You have another advantage over the old mystery school initiates. In those days, ascension was a personal and individual experience. But nowadays, the entire planet is gearing up for a planetary ascension. So that you can all make the necessary changes in a short time, many beings such as myself are paving the way for you to keep pace with the planet's progress. I am here to talk about ascension: your imminent ascension, and not some far distant historical event. I am talking about changes you are already undergoing and which will continue in the coming years. In this book, we'll examine personal and planetary ascension, how it affects you, and how you can make the process go more smoothly. This book is a guide to the new terrain, what you will find, and who you will meet. It introduces you to a new vocabulary which will allow you to converse with your fellow travelers with the minimum of misunderstanding, although you must realize that your particular journey is unique.

I am using this particular channel because he is of my energy, and therefore our frequencies match closely. Also, he has an extensive technical background, and while this book is not at all technical, I require some precision in describing how energy is manipulated. Off the physical plane, the laws of energy are different, but there are still laws and I want to convey a sense of them with clarity.

Use this book as a means for informing your intellect of the process of ascension. Your spirit-self will ensure that the other levels of your being also get the message, because ascension is a "community effort." Your body consciousness and emotional energy are capable of direct cognition without intermediate language. Rest assured that they are getting the message also.

So please read about the process, reflect on it, and discuss it. But do not think for a moment that the written word is all you are getting. At the spirit level, you have all worked with me in the vast Now-point, although you would think of it as a past-life activity. We know each other, and have built up a bond of trust and love over long periods. If you go forward with this book, be aware that knowing its contents alone will change your life and is therefore a commitment to your personal ascension.

This book is a practical guide to a process that is already under way. It is about metaphysics in the true meaning — the physics behind physics — and describes experiments that you can perform in the safety of your own aura. Notice also that it's not called THE Ascension Handbook. It's only one of many such books that are appearing at this point in the process.

The book is in two parts. Part One lays the groundwork and introduces you to energy fields. I have worded it so that no special knowledge is required. We also briefly review the events leading to where your planet is now. Part Two is practical: what you can do to accelerate your personal ascension, and thereby the planetary ascension. Because the planet is really one large energy field, each step you take towards personal ascension not only makes it easier for you, but also for everyone else. You are, therefore, a leader by example.

We know that you've been bombarded with metaphysical books since the printing press was invented, but never before has this type of book been so important. Planetary ascension as fact is not negotiable, and a time frame has been set, one that doesn't leave much time for debate. So please treat this with the same urgency that we who are off the physical plane do. As Lightworkers, you have prepared for this process since you first started to incarnate on this planet. Our purpose here is to guide the final push — your personal ascension.

But, however much we push, a conscious pull is needed on your part. Share this material with your friends, form groups to play with the exercises, talk about ascension to whomever will listen (and to those who won't). It's important that everyone knows what's happening, otherwise we may face mass confusion. You are collectively entering the glorious conclusion of a glorious experiment, and the stage is set. The entire universe is poised in anticipation, so play your parts with joy.

— I am Serapis

Part One ═══════════════════════════════

Ascension: What Is It?

A scension is basically a change in frequency and a change in focus of consciousness. This book looks at energy as the "stuff" behind everything. This energy collaborates and combines in indescribably complex ways to form you, everything you know, and everything you don't know. The two major qualities or characteristics of energy are its amplitude and the rate at which it vibrates, or its frequency.

Your physical body, emotions, thoughts, and spirit are all made of this stuff, blended in ways that make you unique in all the universe. Because the energy you are has frequency, you can change it. That's all ascension is. As you raise the rate of the lowest frequency energy in your physical body, it becomes less dense and incorporates energy of ever higher frequency. As it does, you will see things and think things that were not possible before. You will literally become a fifth-dimensional being, operating on the fifth dimension, working with other fifth-dimensional beings. The low-frequency stuff of fear and limitation will fall away and you will live in a state of what you would today call ecstasy, at one with your spirit and with the spirit of everyone else. That's ascension.

We need to define another term. We will see that, in reality, the notion of your spirit, my spirit, his spirit, her spirit and so on is linear, limiting, and just plain wrong. Once you get beyond the lowest levels of separation of the physical plane, there is just Spirit — an ever changing energy gestalt that has been called God, All That Is, the Source, the Great Spirit, and countless other names. I use the capitalized word "Spirit" for this in cases where separation is unnecessary. In other cases, I use "spirit-self" to denote an individualized portion of Spirit associated with you as an incarnation and with all your co-incarnations across time, plus all the higher-frequency nonphysical levels of your being. But, remember, this is a compromise made for explanation only: there is just Spirit, and I use the two terms interchangeably.

Spirit appears to individuate in order to perform a specific function, such as being you. Spirit operates through the brilliant pinpoint of your consciousness, focused within your physical body. This is the you that knows itself as you, your personality, and is what I term "ego-self." You, the ego-self, are a manifestation of you, the spirit-self, but the peculiar property of the ego-self is that it doesn't know that it is of Spirit — until now, that is!

The term "ego-self" is not used to diminish who you are in any way, but to shift your attention from your outward-looking ego to *who you really are*: an inward-looking focal point within your spirit-self, that in turn is your Spirit function. Or, to put it another way, you are Spirit-in-action.

What is Energy?

Each of you possesses a number of bodies. You are familiar with one of them — the physical body — but less so with the emotional, mental, and spiritual bodies. All these bodies are composed of energy, but the energy is not of the familiar electromagnetic spectrum such as light, radio waves, or X-rays. I speak of the energy behind this familiar energy and behind what you call matter. It is not detectable by your scientists' instruments because they, too, are made of matter, and no instrument can detect frequencies higher than those from which it is made.

This higher-frequency energy is the energy of the Source. It is the energy from which third-dimensional energy such as light is derived. But all energy is a continuum, and for our discussion we could think of it in the form of unimaginable numbers of "units," each of them aware and conscious in their own way. These energy units agree to participate in higher order frameworks of consciousness, such as myself and the cells of your body. Energy forms what you and I are, and its awareness is the basis of our awareness of ourselves; it is what we are made of. In return, our sense of being organizes the energy units, and provides a psychological structure for them in which they can express themselves.

The universe is arranged to allow energy gestalts such as myself to perform function. Any names that we use refer to the function we are performing when we communicate with you, and do not imply any identity within Spirit. Any names used are purely for the convenience of, and communication with, your conscious minds. Although I am aware of myself as pure Spirit energy, I do not regard myself as having an identity other than the function I perform. I am the energy that makes up the gestalt called the Serapis function at this moment, but this energy is constantly shifting and changing.

You can imagine, for the sake of this explanation, that energy is divided into octaves, with the Source as the highest octave and the physical plane as the lowest octave we shall be talking about. I, and other levels of your being, exist and perform our functions in these octaves. Imagine them like several FM radio bands on your radio, with each being such as myself as one particular station. Each band supports a different range of frequencies, and each of us operates in every band. One occupies the same relative position in the dial within each band, getting progressively higher in frequency. Or to use the analogy of a piano keyboard, one is the same relative note in each octave on the keyboard, seven in this case. So if your individual notes, in each of the seven octaves, were sounded together, the result would be the totality of your being — a very beautiful sound.

Remember that these analogies do not even come close to conveying the real story. There are many bands and an infinite number of notes in each. Also, at these levels, you are constantly blending with other energies to perform certain functions.

Not only is my being composed of energy, but anything I conceive of is manifested through further organization of energy units. Whenever I create anything, from an atom to a galaxy, I first project a receptive field analogous to space, and then transmit or radiate energy units into it, organized according to my intent or thoughtforms.

The only way that anything can be created is by organizing this unlimited supply of energy units according to intent. So, the being that I know as myself, plus all that I create or destroy, is composed of energy. Again, this energy is not the heat or light that you know, but a more subtle energy, akin to the energy of a thought that you might have.

This raises many interesting questions about the dimensions of energy such as the nature of space and time.

Space

I said that I project a receptive field, analogous to space, into which I radiate energy units according to my intent. This is a higher order of space than physical space, and in your terms would take up no actual space at all. It is, however, every bit as real to me as the dimensions of a room are to you. I project or imagine this space, as others like me project the three-dimensional space in which you live. You may have heard it said that physical space is nothing more than a thoughtform or an idea construct. This raises the question "Who is doing the thinking?" Rest assured that vast entities are diligently "thinking" your three-dimensional space, maintaining it with a clarity and focus that is beyond description. For many of you, other levels of your own being are part of this.

The space we conceive has a susceptibility or conduciveness to energy, much like a highway is more conducive to vehicles than the terrain on which it is built, or a wire is more conducive to electricity than the surrounding air. Space is therefore a field created to conduct energy. On the higher planes, we create our own space; on the physical plane, other levels of your own being create the physical space in which you live. It is both a unifying and a separating field: unifying in the sense that it allows what we radiate into it to interact, and separating in that it is organized so that the radiations don't overlap. Imagine putting two objects together like a pair of bookends. They don't merge into each other because the type of field we project keeps their fields separate.

Time

From my perspective and from that of other levels of your own being, time as you know it simply doesn't exist. I, and other levels of your being, fully participate in the present, past, and future of this planet simultaneously. I am aware of portions of my energy incarnating at many points in Earth's history with as much intimacy as you have for the incarnation you know as you. This is because I am not restricted by a linear brain but use direct cognition. Therein lies a big difference.

The physical brain operates sequentially with finite time needed to process any sensory input. Without denying its awesome structure, the brain and nervous system are slow. Your finger is burning, so you move it off the stove or drop the hot pan. It could take up to a second between initial contact and letting go. More complex projects, such as designing a new house or computer system, may take months or years, because of the time taken to process thoughts through the brain.

Some projects are so lengthy that they cannot be completed within a participant's lifetime, and so the concept of history came about. Someone being born today has to be informed about what has happened on the planet to date, or at least selected parts of what has happened. Some people spend their entire lives recording what's happening and telling others about it, all because the physical brain synapses take a few milliseconds to fire.

The nonphysical levels of your being do not have this limitation. Through direct cognition of the energy of events, I can tap into any point in what you think of as your planet's history or future with equal ease.

I suggest that you try to visualize what this feels like. Imagine that you are a higher frequency aspect of your own consciousness and are looking down at several people, each in a different period of history. By simple intent, you can merge with any one of them or all of them at once, become them, and know every facet of what they're thinking and feeling, because you are them. You are, say, an Atlantean crystal specialist, a Roman soldier, a medieval peasant, and, of course, the self you know today. Try it. Get a sense of how each of them perceives time, how you perceive time, and how you interact.

Now, it was all carefully planned to be this way from the beginning. It didn't have to be like this, however, and other species in other reality systems do it very differently. Your particular species made a collective decision at a high level of Spirit to literally create the sensation of the passage of time, in order to provide several learning tools. One of them — karma, the law of balance — is based on the concept that if person X affects the life of person Y in any way, then the effect of that must be reciprocated. Thus Y must affect the life of X in the same or similar way to create an energetic balance. Now this is grossly simplified and there are many waivers of this reciprocity, but from the perspective of X and Y on the physical plane, X has to act first, then Y. Some framework was needed to prevent everything happening at the same time; otherwise, X and Y would be unable to sort out apparent cause from effect. The framework chosen was the perception of time. To adopt this linear perception of time, you didn't have to create anything new, but just drop the ability to experience simultaneous time. The construction of the brain that the species chose for the human body built this limitation in perfectly. Of course, from a higher perspective, the actions of X and Y occur simultaneously, the exchange being choreographed through their nonphysical levels.

I have elaborated the point of simultaneous time because it explains why the energy available for creation is unlimited. The same energy unit can be in countless points on the physical timeline with great ease by simply declaring its intent. Energy units can form the Atlantean's crystal cutter, the Roman's sword, and the peasant's hoe simultaneously, and — in view of energy's playful nature — would delight in the irony.

I am talking about your *perception* of time, not the arbitrary division into units of hours, minutes, and seconds. They are just the markings on your measuring stick and have little to do with your perception of time. Now, clock time seems very real to you, based — as it appears to be — on the motion of the planet around the sun. There is no real reason why you should organize your activities according to light and dark — it's just convenient. It's also convenient to have the planet rotate around the sun, balancing centripetal and centrifugal forces. By perception of time, I mean how you sense duration and how you perceive one event and then another and then another.

If you could experience all events at once, time would present no sensory obstruction or limitation to you. Imagine a large tapestry made of vertical and horizontal threads. Each vertical thread is one perceived now-point and the horizontal threads represent space. The colored diagonal threads making up the tapestry pattern are the events of your life occurring in time and space. Now, imagine a tiny insect crawling about on the tapestry. If it went horizontally, it would experience each now-point in succession but would be stuck in one place. Occasionally it would stumble over a colored thread and experience a tiny piece of your life. Now, if it went vertically up the tapestry, it would move through space but be stuck in one now-point, and so would experience everything that happens across space but only in one moment. It would see "snapshots" of everything that happened on the planet at one instant, including an instant of your life. Obviously, if our insect gets smart, it follows one of the millions of colored threads and experiences the life of one person.

From your vantage point "outside," you could see the entire tapestry: time, space, and the webwork of people's lives, and could, if you wished, drop in at any point and experience their lives with them. But you'd be too busy because you'd notice that there are millions of tapestries alongside this one, stretching back to infinity and the colored threads actually go from tapestry to tapestry, weaving in three dimensions — the parallel universes that we've heard about. And more: you can faintly see ghost tapestries shimmering about the physical versions — the tapestries of the upper planes. Is someone watching you, just like you were watching the insect as it moved about the tapestry with its head down, diligently following one little thread?

Motion

The two components of space and time lead to a third — motion. To move between two points on the physical plane takes time. Historically, it took months to travel between the east and west coasts of America. Now it takes six hours. The physical plane has a theoretical limit of the speed of light. At this speed, you could cross the country in a sixtieth of a second. But motion is a physical-plane phenomenon only, and does not occur in the same way on higher planes. This is because space is a created field; points in that field are not really separated by anything, and everything exists on top of everything else. Your scientists are puzzled about how two electrons in different places seem to communicate instantaneously. The reason for this is that the conscious energy that manifests as subatomic particles is not "in space" at all. The energy exists in the brilliant One-point, that is, the mind of All That Is, and projects images that appear to be subatomic particles. Because the electrons are projected from the same One-point, it's not surprising that they each know what the other is doing.

Time is simply the perceived duration needed to move between two points, which is zero off the physical plane because all points coexist simultaneously. Because time is simultaneous off the physical plane, if you were an "electron" (i.e. Spirit functioning as an electron), you could project to point A and point B at the same time, so the idea of motion between A and B has no meaning.

I hope that I've conveyed the sense that the underpinnings of the physical plane (space, time, and motion) are in fact arbitrary local laws, applicable to the physical plane frequencies of Earth, and that it's your senses that create the perception of them. Sensing space and time are functions of the intellect and were built into the brain to support the human species on this planet. They are teaching tools just like — in your schools — all students agree (usually) to assemble in one room at a particular time for a lesson on an agreed-upon subject.

In the same way, at the physical level, all members of the species must agree on certain things in order for the "field trip" to planet Earth to be meaningful. And I use the term "field trip" intentionally. It's important that you widen your perceptions to the point where you're aware of yourself as a vast being, on a visit to this corner of the universe, who arranges little "outings"— each one a physical incarnation for which you put on a different body and personality to make it interesting. The outings may be pleasurable or — if you forget who you are — unpleasant, but you certainly learn a lot on each one!

In the next chapter, we go more deeply into the nature of physical matter as a standing wave of the lowest octave of energy, in order to demonstrate the fluidity of what you take for granted as "solid."

In turn, these building blocks of conscious energy then collaborate further to form atoms of a particular element such as carbon, hydrogen, oxygen, nitrogen, etc. An atom may appear to be a very simple construct — electrons rotating around a central nucleus — and in one sense it is. But in another sense, it is the most complex thing on the physical plane. The geometry and algebra that went into the design of the physical plane's atoms would keep most of your largest computers busy for centuries. Matter didn't just happen. It was carefully planned and we had to know how matter would behave under all circumstances before we went ahead with its creation.

Do not think for a moment that the consciousness projecting the electron is tiny. The electron is not a tiny particle but a "probability field" — a part of space in which the consciousness exists, but in such a subtle way that scientists cannot be sure, so they say the electron "probably" exists. That consciousness can collaborate in countless fields in countless universes simultaneously.

Atoms may remain free or bond together to form molecules. Molecules then bond together to form the shape determined jointly by the energy units themselves and the organizing entity. Beings take responsibility for directing energy in the form of atoms or molecules, according to patterns for a crystal or rock, for a cell in a plant seed or a tree, and so on. The list is endless, of course, but the patterns are rather like personal computers. They are both living programs and databases simultaneously, and can store vast amounts of information. The DNA structure at the heart of every one of your body's cells is a database, containing the history of you and your co-incarnations, plus that of the entire species.

For example, a tree grows under the guidance of an energy being — call it a tree-spirit if you like — which conceives the tree "blueprint" and organizes energy units accordingly. Once organized, the energy "remembers" its function and continuously maintains the subatomic particles, arranged in ever larger patterns. When you look at the tree, you are really seeing pure energy organized into a pattern by a conscious, aware being. Your brain decodes this visual energy pattern as "tree" through habit. When you touch the tree, your hand and the tree are two energy fields touching, but your nervous system puts all this information together and decodes the contact as tactile stimulation. Your brain then uses all available data to build the overall construction you know as a tree.

If a carpenter then comes along and chops down the tree and uses the wood to make a chair, he alters the shape of the largest field. The conscious energy units making up the wood "remember" their new pattern and faithfully maintain it until something else happens such as burning the chair. Then the conscious energy of the cellulose molecules repatterns itself, into free carbon, oxygen, and nitrogen atoms, for example.

Just to introduce an idea of scale, the space within and between these atoms is vast. If an atom were the size of a football stadium, the nucleus would be about the size of a football in the center of the stadium. The first ring of electrons would be out around the first row of seats, and each ring of electrons might be fifty rows apart. The next nearest atom may be as far away as the next city, so when we talk about "solid" matter, it's far from solid. And those electrons you think of as little particles have no weight at all. They are just packets of energy whizzing around the nucleus at an enormous speed. It's their speed that gives them apparent substance or a pre-materialistic stage, just like a speeding bullet has more impact than one just thrown at you.

Even the nucleus isn't solid. It, too, is made up of smaller particles (neutrons and protons) which, on closer examination, also turn out to be made up of still smaller particles. At this level, we are approaching the point at which pure energy manifests as what you think of as matter, and the infinitesimally short time periods that this takes. We're also close to the limits of physical instruments. They can detect the sudden appearance of a subatomic particle but not its actual transformation from pure energy, because the energy unit that created it is nonphysical energy and this does not register on physical instruments.

Physicists have concluded that the only time subatomic particles are actually particles is when they observe them, and that the rest of the time they are waves of energy. So researchers can never know the condition of an unobserved electron, and there is, therefore, no way to determine the basic structure of the physical plane or explain its workings.

At a deeper level, we're talking about conscious energy bursting into the physical plane and then flying around at enormous speeds, giving the appearance of solidity, just like the blades of a electric fan in motion look like a solid disk. So, is the material universe just an illusion? Yes. It's all done by holograms and standing waves.

The basis of all organization of energy into matter is the standing wave. This idea is vital to understanding what you are and how you manifest. What follows may sound a little like physics, but it's at the heart of metaphysics.

Holograms

If you're familiar with the phenomenon known as the hologram, you know that the image of an object can be captured on special film by combining two laser beams, one reflected off the object and the other not. These two beams interact, or interfere, with each other to create a special image on the film. When a laser beam is again passed through the film, a three-dimensional image of the original object appears, "floating" in thin air. However, unlike photographic film images, the holographic film image is nothing like the original object, but looks like sets of concentric circles, called interference patterns. And if the laser beam is shone through even a fragment of the film, the image still appears, although less clearly. Thus the image is dispersed over the entire film. There are two aspects here: the object's image caught on film, and the image that's projected.

The analogy of the hologram offers some important clues about the nature of reality, and how you can work with it. On the one hand, we have the daily reality you experience (the explicate, *projected* image pattern), and on the other, we have the blueprint for that reality (the implicit pattern), that is hidden from you. This explains why a subatomic particle can be everywhere at once — its blueprint is dispersed throughout the implicit pattern. This directly contradicts classical physics which describes the physical world as a set of discrete, local things, all busy interacting in very limited ways.

Now we're getting somewhere. Suppose that matter as you know it is made up of subatomic waves, projected out to form three-dimensional wave patterns. That miraculous organ, the human brain, detects these projected patterns and constructs what looks to you like an objective reality from them. And this reality looks real and solid to you because your physical body is also a three-dimensional projected image!

Reality is not, therefore, an objective "out there," but a subjective "in here," and is different for everyone. So what does that make you? Are you explicit flesh and bone, anchored in a solid world, or are you an implicit blur of holographic patterns playing in a vast swirl of larger patterns? And what is the role of consciousness in all this? Is it the light shining through the hidden patterns on the film, or is it the pattern itself? It is both. Consciousness both forms the hidden blueprints from even more remote blueprints, and shines the light through them to project what you see, feel, and hear. But we're talking about different functions here. Subatomic consciousness creates the building blocks of matter, and other parts of consciousness organize them in ever more complex patterns — your cells, physical organs, emotions, and thoughts, all of which are fully conscious in their own way. And your consciousness interacts with every other consciousness, be it living or so-called "inanimate."

I know that this is enough to blow the fuses in anyone's mental body, but it's important to know how fluid reality is, in order to be able to manipulate it. If you believed that you were somehow fixed in your makeup, you might not give yourself permission to change. For example, you know that you have lots of old behavior patterns stored in the cells of your physical body. If these cells were "frozen," and this old energy was locked in, how could you ever release it? But if your cells are projections from some hidden blueprint, what if you could change the blueprint or how it was projected? And you have just the tool to do it: consciousness.

As we'll see later, the human species is on a quest — a reality creation quest — but you've gotten so good at reality creation that you don't know you're doing it any more. Everything you experience is a direct result of your efforts at reality creation and a faithful projection of the inner blueprints. If you don't know that you're doing this, or that you can change the blueprint, you'll keep creating the same old reality, and that's no fun. But things are far more malleable and plastic than you realize, and this is going to prove very important later on.

Your emotions and thoughts are part of the inner blueprint, and your daily life is the projected image. Of course, your emotions and thoughts interact with those of everyone else, just as you share your life with everyone else, but what you think and feel play a very large part in what happens to you.

Reality, as you know it, is projected from a variety of hologram-like blueprints. The blueprints exist at various levels of "removedness" from ordinary reality, and the images they project overlap. The lowest frequency images appear solid to your solid body, but what you think of as space is full of higher-frequency images, all coexisting. You yourself consist of many projections — physical, emotional, mental, and spiritual — from blueprints devised by you, as Spirit. And these blueprints are in turn projections from higher-frequency, more removed blueprints. What's important here is that you can modify these blueprints through visualization. If you're sick, you can use visualization to "repair" the blueprint and regain health. If you want to bring about a situation, you can design a new blueprint and sit back as it is projected into the physical plane as events that you then experience.

Reality creation works both ways, however. If you're in a situation you don't like, yet are resisting it rather than visualizing something else, you are reinforcing both the blueprint and the projection mechanism, thus perpetuating the unwanted situation.

So, consciousness is the pattern behind objective reality and everything in the history of planet Earth, and consciousness lies deep within the fabric of reality.

Any of you who follow the TV series *Star Trek: The Next Generation* have an excellent model for reality creation. The holodeck on the Enterprise is able to generate images of objects and people, which operate within the parameters specified by the person programming the "reality." A subtle change in the program can cause a change in, say, a holographic character's aggression level, or defuse a threatening situation. Unlike today's holograms, however, a holographic bullet will kill you and a holographic monster can devour you, unless you stop the program first. The TV series is set in the 24th century, but the technology to sculpt energy in this way will be available long before then.

This brings us to how the physical plane is actually formed. A holographic image is formed by light being held in an envelope that is a representation of the original. All the information needed to generate the image is encoded in the film. The envelope is actually a kind of standing wave.

Standing Waves

As a child, you've probably held a string taut with a friend and plucked it. A little wave zips down the string, hits your friend's hand and comes back to you. It's energy that's moving along the string. The string moves up and down but not lengthwise.

If you both pluck the string at the same time, two things can happen. You get a double-sized wave in the middle if you both plucked the string the same way, or the two waves cancel out if one of you plucked up and the other down. The two waves interfere with each other, constructively in the first case and destructively in the second.

Now imagine a shorter string, held taut like a guitar string. Pluck this and it makes a characteristic sound. What you did by plucking it was introduce raw energy into it. This energy naturally falls into certain patterns. The strongest pattern is a wave which has a wavelength the same as the string's length, say three feet. Other waves also form, and they have wavelengths of a half, a third, a quarter, etc. of the string's length. This gives waves of, say, eighteen, twelve, and nine inches in length. These waves are called standing waves and form a family based on the natural wavelength. The particular combination of standing waves is what gives an instrument its individual timbre, or sound signature.

The important thing about our vibrating strings is that two identical strings under identical conditions will always generate the same natural and harmonic waves. And put two identical strings next to each other and pluck one. The plucked string puts out a field of sound energy which the other picks up. Because the second string is tuned exactly to the wavelengths that the first is generating, the second resonates in sympathy very readily. This resonance is supremely important in dealing with human energy bodies, and we'll have much more to say about it in the remainder of this book.

Now we get tricky. Suppose that you're the dessert chef on a spacecraft, and you can make freestanding jello in your zero-gravity kitchen. It just holds together without a container. Suppose you make two kinds of jello — red and yellow. Just before they finally set, you somehow push them together so that they partially merge to form orange jello where they meet. Now, if you poked the red one and made it wobble, the wobble would pass right through to the yellow one. If you poked the red one regularly to set up a standing wave, the yellow one, being made of exactly the same stuff, would resonate at the same frequency. And imagine what would happen if you were clever enough to create the yellow one inside the red one. Think how the yellow jello would react.

You've just discovered an innate quality of fields and the phenomenon of standing wave resonance between two fields — that is, if a field is tuned to energy of a particular frequency, it will absorb the energy of a standing wave in another field and will create a standing wave of its own. Quite dispassionately and automatically, any field will begin to resonate with the energy of a similar field in its vicinity. This can produce sympathetic resonance that could be detrimental. The first field could be moved in a way that is against its own best interests. Well done. All you need to do now is to find a way to eat jello in a weightless environment!

As we'll see, resonance affects *you* in countless ways, whether you know about it or not. But from now on, you will be able to use it consciously as an ascension tool.

Energy Fields

Your personality consists of three energy fields, along with their contents. I call the combination of a field and its energy a "body." Out of its own energy, your spirit-self projects or manifests three fields: the physical, the emotional, and the mental. Energy is arranged in standing waves within an envelope to form the three energy bodies. A fourth body — the spiritual body — forms a bridge between these lower three bodies and Spirit. The fact that they are manifested out of the same "stuff" as your spirit body is of supreme importance, as we'll see later.

Let's deal with the physical body first. Many factors determine how it manifests. Long ago, the human species decided to opt for a physical birth process rather than simply projecting the body into a field created by Spirit (we'll see why later). Also, conception was devised as a means of diversifying the gene pool to allow for infinite variety in the physical genetic blueprints.

At the moment of your conception, two complete DNA blueprints were merged to form a third. As the egg divided and cells formed, conscious energy units collaborated to form subatomic particles, then atoms and molecules. This process was guided by patterns held in your DNA — the overall blueprint for your particular physical body.

You, as Spirit, carefully crafted your DNA from that of your parents. You had selected your future parents for their genetics and the kind of imprinting and family circumstances that you wanted for your incarnation-to-be. In collaboration with their spirit-selves, the three of you decided the moment of conception, based on some very complex factors. (Astrologers have glimpsed just a tiny part of the complexity!)

Scientists have decoded only a fraction of the millions of pieces of information stored in the DNA. In addition to your physical characteristics, your DNA also contains your entire incarnational history across time, plus the history of every species that has ever lived and will ever live. You can look at DNA as a series of protein molecules, but, like a hologram, it should be read in its totality for maximum effect.

During the first few months of gestation, the conscious energy forming your cells reads the DNA, decoding it to find out what kind of cell it should build. The growing cells, also conscious in their own way, tune into the blueprint for the physical body and the simultaneous "future" for guidance in how to grow. They organize themselves, pulling in more energy units to manifest as the necessary types of atoms, and multiply within the overall envelope specified in the DNA for their particular function. The consciousness of a cell which opts to be a liver cell, for example, pulls in energy and splits to form other liver cells. As your physical development proceeds, they multiply within the ever-growing standing wave established for the liver. Growth is fast in the beginning and slows down toward the end of gestation. Growth continues for several years and eventually settles down to a replacement-only basis.

So, your physical body is built of standing waves within standing waves within standing waves as your emerging body consciousness formed atoms, molecules, cells, and organs under the guidance of your spirit-self and a kind of "future" version of your body, which acted as a blueprint.

Once created and grown to full size, your physical body is not left to run down like some clockwork machine. The energy making up the particles of your body is refreshed several million times a second. Your body is, in effect, recreated constantly, according to the blueprints in your DNA and the mental blueprint thoughtforms you hold about your body.

Your body is a miraculous entity with a consciousness of its own, and regulates itself superbly. But it looks to the larger you for much of its input. Through resonance, the thoughts and emotions you hold about yourself have an enormous impact on your body consciousness, and a fear of disease and death will quite literally program your body for illness. Equally, thoughts of good health, joy of living, and so on, will program your body to unleash its own healing powers. These powers will deal with cellular DNA corruption (often the cause of cancers) and conditions normally attributed to aging.

This explanation doesn't even begin to touch on the complexity of what actually happens. Even the briefest reflection on how you grow your body would put you in awe of yourself. This cursory coverage is intended to show only that the body you think of as solid is actually energy arranged in a series of standing waves, which appear to your physical senses as a continuum of subatomic particles, atoms, molecules, cells, and organs, and finally the entire body. Each unit of energy is fully aware of its role and gladly collaborates in the structure you know as your body, according to your pictures of reality.

It may surprise you to learn that your body is conscious, but not conscious as you understand the term. Your body knows, for example, how to beat its heart, digest food, and heal itself. It is aware of the cycles of the moon, the planets, and the stars, and constantly uses these cycles and adapts to them. After all, it is composed of aware energy taken from the vast planetary field. In this sense, the planet and Spirit played a far greater role in your birth than did your biological parents!

What you think of as your consciousness is actually a blend of several different types of consciousness (although they comprise a unity underneath it all):

◆ Subatomic consciousness, aware of the vast cosmic fields in which it interacts with all other subatomic consciousness

◆ Cellular consciousness, based on DNA blueprints, and impressed with the experiences of your life, your thoughts, and emotions

◆ Body consciousness, or the gestalt of cellular consciousness, plus a few ideas of its own (the body relies largely on the mental body's beliefs for its self-image, however)

◆ Emotions that flow through you in the moment, overlaid with past emotions that you held onto instead of allowing them to flow

◆ Thoughts and beliefs that you use to structure reality (Be aware that any belief is only an opinion about reality.)

◆ Spiritual consciousness, intuition, or direct cognition. This aspect taps into what's often been called Universal Mind. It's actually part of a hidden blueprint from which reality flows and contains, among other things, your species' archetypes — the heroic aspects of humanity. Through this "connective tissue" for physical reality, you can access other times, other places, and other dimensions.

Now most of the energy making up your physical body is assimilated from food you take in, but increasingly, that energy is becoming projected. Here's how it works: the Spirit levels of your being project conscious energy units into your physical field and direct them to form the cellular structures, rather than using the energy of proteins, starches, and so on from digested food. Your spirit-self is systematically converting the cells of your body to being fueled by projected energy rather than by digested energy. This projected energy is derived from the energy behind the radiation which you know as light. As a result, you are beginning to form what is often called a "Light Body." Your physical body is being progressively more and more sustained by energy than by physical nutrients held in a cellular envelope. One effect of this is that the frequency of your cells and of your overall body is rising. Eventually your body will begin to glow gently. At that point, you will be in a Light Body. This change is initiated in several different ways, but usually requires some form of conscious consent on your part. This book is intended to provide a roadmap of the terrain ahead so that you can commit to this process with knowledge and understanding. (In an excellent little book, *What Is Lightbody?*, channeled by Tachi-ren, Archangel Ariel presents a 12-level model of the process of going to Light, and the physical, emotional, and mental symptoms of each level.)

Your various fields (emotional, mental, and spiritual) rotate with a frequency that is characteristic for you. Some people spin quickly, others slowly. But you spin each field in a specific ratio to the other fields — 11, 22, 33, and so on. If the spin rate of one field changes and the ratio changes, you may feel "out of sorts" or dizzy. Field spin and the relative rates of spin are vitally important, and we'll return to them in Part Two.

To close this chapter, it's often been said that science and religion are like two railroad trains moving in the same direction on parallel tracks, with religion looking for the Thinker and science looking for the Thought. They will soon come to a switch where the two tracks become one. What will happen? There could be a terrible wreck or they could realize that the Thinker and the Thought are one. The organizing principle of the universe and the energy from which the physical and nonphysical universe is made are the same thing: a continuum of aware energy of every conceivable and inconceivable frequency, organized with breathtaking beauty, and delighting in the exhilaration of creativity. In the next chapter, we take a closer look at this energy.

3

Energy Fields

Look carefully at the book you are reading. Many types of energy contribute to make up this object. First, an envelope or field-space is necessary. A standing wave defines this field, literally making the space in which it exists more conducive to energy manifestation.

At the other end of the scale, the standing wave of each atom is a field about one hundred-millionth of a centimeter across. Billions of these atoms make up the molecules of the paper and ink, again forming standing waves. Some are organized in strands of cellulose and other organic and inorganic chemicals. Their fields actually extend outward to infinity. However, the book-shaped envelope is an area of higher conductivity space, and the space outside the book field is less conducive to this energy, so the intensity of the energy drops sharply at the field boundary but does not cease entirely.

Within the field envelope generated for the book, the energy is supported as it bursts through a barrier to form semi-physical subatomic particles. These densify to make the atoms of the paper and ink. Thus billions of conscious energy units collaborate in a material manifestation as envisioned by myself, the channel, the publisher, and then by you, the reader. So your role is as vital as mine in co-creating and maintaining this book. Your eyes and brain decode the swirling patterns of energy held in various envelopes, and in a miracle of organization, you find yourself reading this book. Of course, all this happens well outside your conscious mind. How could you ever concentrate enough to read this or any book if you consciously had to remember to keep thinking it into existence?

So the book you have in your hands consists of energy of a variety of frequencies ranging from those that make up subatomic particles to the larger waves that define paper size. And it also contains another frequency: mine. The ink is arranged in symbols (letters and words) used to convey my meaning, and these symbols have a characteristic frequency over and above that of the ink used. The processes by which my meanings are encoded in these symbols, and by which you decode them to extract my meaning, are phenomenally complex. You may dismiss it as "just reading," but it would take an entire volume to even begin to describe this process, even if we had a language to express it. On top of that, the very high frequency associated with my function uses the opportunity of you sitting down to read this book to impart much more information into your fields than you consciously absorb from reading this book.

Physical Fields

Now, we saw earlier that your body is composed of aware energy which knows that it's making up the cells in your body. We've also seen that this energy has a field which stretches to infinity, but that its intensity diminishes outside the standing wave field that contains it. So, although your energy level is very strong within the envelope of your physical body, your personal fields extend far beyond the envelope of your skin.

This extended field is both a transmitter and a receiver. With it, you can sense potential harm long before it comes close to you. So-called "instinct" is actually your extended fields detecting another field, be it of a hungry tiger or a runaway truck. Similarly, you transmit energetic signals via your extended field for others to pick up, hence the adage that fear is contagious. Some people are more powerful transmitters and more sensitive receivers than others, but you all do this, without exception. It's what Ariel calls "being a bio-transducer."

Emotional Fields

We saw earlier that your spirit-self actually manifests three fields: physical, emotional, and mental. Your emotional field is composed of energy that does not burst through the physical barrier into subatomic particles as does physical field energy. Obviously it interacts with your physical field because you feel emotions in your body, and your emotions directly affect the state of your physical body, for better or worse. It is, however, an entirely separate field with a larger envelope — say, two to six feet beyond the body's surface perimeter, but it can be much larger in some people.

Your emotional body is a field through which energies of particular frequencies run. You generate some of these yourself, and you pick up others using your field as an antenna. So, a particular emotion can be communicated. It is important that you know, first, which energy you generate and which you pick up, and second, that you have control over the energy you allow in your emotional field.

Suppose that you suddenly feel angry. Where did this anger come from? Of course, something within you may have triggered it, such as an expectation that another person would behave in a certain way and he or she didn't, or that a situation would turn out a certain way and it didn't. The fact that your plans are thwarted results in feeling helpless, and the energy of enthusiasm you had is now stifled within the emotional field. You then feel it as anger.

Alternatively, anger may spring apparently from nowhere. In this case, you may be picking up anger from someone who just happens to be in your field. The anger isn't yours and you can dump it very easily. You can spin your emotional field to centrifuge it out, declaring that you release the energy back to the universe. Feel it drain away.

Releasing your own internal anger is almost as easy. But first, you must realize that it is only energy and that energy loves to move. It hates being still. Also, realize that this energy is not yours, but only on loan for the moment. Spin your fields and declare to yourself:

"This anger (or fear, jealousy, etc.) is not me or mine. I release it back to the universe."

Emotional energy is neither good or bad; it just is. However, you may prefer not to remove some frequencies like love or joy from your field. If an emotion feels good to you, you are picking the energy up from another source: Spirit.

Mental Fields

The third field is the home of the intellect and operates in yet a higher frequency band than the emotional, with a higher rate of spin. Any thought you think is composed of organized energy and has its reality in that energy. Thoughts, therefore, are energy structures in your mental field, making up your mental body. This, too, is derived from a hidden blueprint, the source of those great ideas that "just come to you." A thought is a real thing, but your scientists are just not able to measure it yet, although several projects are coming close (many experiments have detected changes in leaf conductivity when an experimenter approaches a living plant with pruning shears and ill intent!). A thought is high-frequency energy organized in a coherent structure. You transmit your thoughts out from your mental field just like you do from the other fields, but not as many people can pick up your thoughts as can pick up physical and emotional energies.

The clarity of a thoughtform's structure depends directly on the clarity of conception. A radio station playing an old, crackly record will faithfully transmit old, crackly music. This is important because the thoughtforms you transmit directly affect all the fields around you. So if you are thinking clear but fearful thoughts, you are transmitting a very clear signal that you expect something bad to happen, and boosting it with fuel from accompanying fearful emotions. The universe is very accommodating in that regard and will rearrange itself to deliver. You have literally changed the energy fields around you by transmitting fear-based thoughtforms into them. Others will pick up your fearful thoughtforms, usually unknowingly, and see you as a "victim waiting to happen." You are literally inviting them to reinforce your victim mentality, and they may oblige. Alternatively, if you see yourself as divinely protected, someone looking for a victim will not notice you because the two of you do not resonate. But you will be noticed by others who *do* resonate to your field. That's how you create your own reality. It's all done by resonance, which is impartial to "good" and "bad" energy alike.

So, just like the two guitar strings exchanging standing wave energy, other people will pick up your fear, amplify it, and play it back to you. One fearful person in a group can "amp up" the fear in everyone around them, and soon the fearful person may *really* have something to be afraid of! Fortunately, the emotional energy of love and love-filled thoughtforms transmit and resonate in exactly the same way, only more so, because they are in harmony with the nature of the universe, and things always go more easily if they are in the flow.

Add to this two other factors: you are becoming a more powerful transmitter and the universe is becoming increasingly more malleable and susceptible to your thoughtforms. These two factors work to shorten the time needed to manifest your thoughts. Previously you had to hold a belief for years for it to manifest in your life, but increasingly it now takes only days. Fortunately, beliefs that are consistent with the flow of the universal truth manifest more easily than those that go against the grain.

Your Mind Is Not Your Brain

Many scientists are busy looking inside the brain for the functions of the human mind. This is like looking inside a radio set for the voice and wondering how the electronic circuitry is smart enough to know the stock market prices, where the freeway bottlenecks are, what the weather forecast is, and all the other things you hear on the radio.

Obviously the radio doesn't really know these things, but what it does do very well is to detect an electromagnetic field that is coded with this information — the broadcast signal to which it's tuned. Similarly the brain detects some of what goes on in the mental field. It is only limited by habit in what it can pick up, and you can easily stretch it a little. You have a "favorite station" that you listen to all the time, but with a little practice, you can easily move up and down the dial. Some of you do this unknowingly and get very confused by all the weird broadcasts and static put out by other people.

The brain itself knows nothing, of course. It's a miraculous decoder and translator, and an amazingly complex antenna into the mental and physical fields. It processes signals from your outer senses and correlates them to give you a composite picture of physical reality. When your eyes see an energy pattern, your brain converts the jumble of signals into images of tables, chairs, trees, and so on. But the functions of the mind *per se*, like the act of thinking, reside firmly in your mental field, not in your brain.

Do not think that I am belittling the brain. As a biotransducer component, it is one of the most complex electro-chemical energy transmitter/receivers on any physical plane, anywhere. You, as Spirit, developed it in response to the human species' call for a brilliant focus in the physical plane. It is unique within the universe.

So, what you think of as "you" is actually a number of fields, each one a supporting medium for a band of amazingly complex energies comprised of an enormous number of interacting frequencies. This combination of energies, or energetic signature, defines your personality and is unique in the universe. These indescribably complex patterns that make up the you that you know are constantly changing, according to the moment-by-moment shifts in the intentions and functions of your spirit-self. I urge you to become sensitive to your energy, and if you're busy doing something and suddenly it doesn't seem like fun anymore, then stop and do something else, or do nothing. The change you felt signalled a higher-dimensional shift and the energy just dropped out of whatever you were doing. Similarly, you may be in a certain place and suddenly you feel that you must get out. Honor that feeling and leave. Don't apologize; just say "I've got to go now."

Although the energies in your physical, emotional, and mental fields do not overlap in frequency, extremely complex resonances occur between them. For example, the energy of fear in your emotional body will stifle optimistic thoughts in your mental body. Energy also interacts within a particular body. For example, a frequency of fear automatically dampens and possibly excludes the frequency of love, because of the way that they interact. Fear — be it manifesting as suspicion, jealousy, arrogance, self-deprecation, or whatever — consists of low-frequency energy that blocks higher frequency energy. Do not judge fear as bad — it is a good teacher of some lessons — but I urge you to see it for what it is: just energy. It's always based on a sense of inadequacy or a feeling of being unable to cope with life or some aspect of it, and, ultimately, on a sense of being separate from Spirit (note that it's only a *sense* of separation. You are never actually separate nor ever could be — that's not how the universe works).

Fear can be of such high amplitude that it swamps your entire field, and actually distorts all emotions and thoughts. With this distorted perception, you interpret even acts of kindness toward you as, say, others' self-interest. Fortunately, as we shall see, the emotion of love acts in the same way, and can swamp all three fields.

Probably the thing that most determines how you feel and how well you function is the degree of alignment between these bodies (remember that a body is the combination of a field and its contents). When you're aligned, your bodies are symmetrically positioned around your physical body and are spinning at the rates that are best for you. After a big row with someone, your emotional body may be literally "bent out of shape," or after some intense brainwork, your mental body may only be located around your head and spinning erratically. Later on, we'll look at some techniques for realigning your bodies, but for now, it's enough just to know that you've got them.

The Chakra System

How does energy in these fields actually resonate if the three fields are in different frequency bands and spinning at different rates? That's where the chakras come in. They are frequency transformers for energy and little storehouses in their own right.

There are many accounts of the chakras, but few actually tell you what they do. Suppose something big is happening in one field — say, a massive influx of sexual energy because you're about to make love. The second chakra in this case is especially tuned to this frequency and translates the energy in the field that is excited (spiritual, mental, or emotional) into frequencies that turn the other fields on. As a result, all three fields start buzzing with love-making energy.

Or, if your survival was threatened, the first chakra would pick up the thought of danger from the mental field or the feeling of anger in the emotional field of someone approaching you. It would broadcast "DANGER!" through the other fields and, if you are in alignment, you would respond very quickly. If the energy in your fields is not in alignment, you become confused. Your mental body thinks "I'll talk him out of it," your emotional body feels "I remember this from when I was little," and your physical body says "Run for it!"

We are grateful to Ariel for bringing a technique onto the planet called the Unified Chakra. In this process, you literally expand your heart chakra to encompass all the others. As we'll see in Part Two, the unified chakra and aligned energy fields are very important, not just for survival, but — more importantly — as vital tools for ascension.

Thus, at one level, you are made up of three fields, each consisting of energy of countless different frequencies. Each field carries or supports energy of particular frequencies in standing waves, and acts as both a transmitter and a receiver antenna.

The blend of frequencies and relative amplitudes is uniquely yours and, to a large extent, defines who you are as a body and a personality. This blend, or energy signature, is yours in the same way that the timbre of a particular instrument distinguishes it from all others, even of the same type. The energy of the three bodies interacts in indescribably complex ways. Your thoughts affect your physical and emotional fields, and your emotions affect your thoughts and physical body.

We saw earlier that your set of fields resonates with two other types of field: the fields of other people around you and the planet-wide fields of the consensus reality. Each person you meet is running his or her own energy show. Suppose one day you're out walking about town, feeling good, positive, confident, free of fear, and in love with the world. You meet an old friend who's just been fired and is worried and/or angry. What's going to happen when your fields merge on the street corner?

Your friend's emotional body is transmitting fear and his mental body is transmitting negative thoughtforms, and your fields are picking them up. Any fear frequency energy in you starts to hum and a standing wave may begin to build. You are transmitting into your friend's fields, also, and maybe some higher frequency energy begins to resonate in him or her. The actual outcome would have been unpredictable before now, but you know about this stuff now. You are *not* responsible for what happens in your friend's fields, even though you know what's going on. You are, however, totally responsible for what's happening in *your* fields. Meeting a miserable friend and becoming miserable through resonance is not mastery (unless, of course, you really want a good cry to dump some grief from your cells). You are responsible if you let resonance creep up on you. Part Two contains some tricks for detecting standing waves in others and for shielding yourself from their effects.

This kind of situation is easy to spot and deal with compared with the second type of field — the planetary consensus reality. This is much more difficult because you're fully immersed in it, like a fish in water. You only notice air when it's full of fog or pollution. The field containing consensus reality energy is far less evident than that, especially when you've lived in it all your life. It forms a huge sphere around and within the planet, much like air, although much less beneficial.

Every time you inhale or exhale, you exchange some of the air you share with everyone else on this planet. Each time you think a thought or feel an emotion, you also exchange energy with the consensus reality. And you don't have to do a thing. Just sitting quietly at home, you are immersed in the stuff, just like the radio waves from all the radio stations are flooding your body at this moment. And I warn you — the 1990s are going to be rough, as people plunge into the last remaining years to dump the garbage from their fields and clear karma with others and themselves. So the last thing you want to do is to tune into the "consensus channel" — it only shows horror movies.

Dropping the habit of watching television news and being very selective about newspapers is an excellent idea. When you can't tell the difference between the news and a crime drama, it's time to switch it off. And the news will get more, rather than less, bizarre as people demand to know that some other poor guy out there has got it worse than they have.

Now, I'm not suggesting that you become callous about other people starring in the karmic horror movies that they call their lives, but if they believe that they are victims of a random universe, and that it's only a matter of time before an airplane crashes through their roof or a runaway bus comes through their wall, they are creating a reality that you don't want to share. Very soon, you will find that you just don't *resonate* with people like that and that you're gravitating to the company of other masters.

If you accept that the universe is benign, and that your spirit-self is there to assist in the ascension process, you won't be swamped by the "I may be next" energy of the consensus reality. Again, Part Two contains a few tricks for unplugging from the sticky consensus reality and plugging into the glorious reality that Spirit is manifesting on your planet.

Planet Earth is unique in its density and the personality's severed perceptions of Spirit. Nowhere, on any planet, has densification and separation from Spirit gone as deeply as it has on Earth. You collectively pulled off a brave experiment to see just how far from the Source you could go. The good news is that the experiment has been a brilliant success and is now over. It's time to dismantle the apparatus and go home. So, let's take a look at how all this started. How did it all happen?

4

The Origin of the Species

I said earlier — and this is probably the most important statement in this book — that "Your true nature is Spirit." The you that you think of as "you" is just one of many, projected across time and in various places on this and other planets in universes you haven't discovered yet. Now this in no way belittles who you perceive yourself to be. On the contrary, you are a vast, multi-dimensional being, a magnificent expression of the Source, which you brilliantly and lovingly crafted to perform your spirit function. Nowhere, on any planet in any universe, has such a creation as you existed. And just knowing that you are part of a much larger enterprise can immeasurably increase the sense of your life's meaningfulness.

As this truly awesome being, you decided that, for a very special purpose, you would incarnate on this planet at this exciting time in its history. The result of that is, of course, the "you" of which you are aware. Never take for granted the brilliant pinpoint of consciousness, focused in the here and now, that you are. If you had any idea of the process by which you existed, you would be in awe of your own power. So, please try to see yourself as Spirit having a human experience, and not the other way around.

You may ask, "If I really am this vast being, how come I don't know about it or sense it in some way?" Well, just stop reading for a moment and try to sense your larger self as a force, supreme and unstoppable, impelling itself into three-dimensional reality as a huge energy wedge, with you as the leading edge. Try to sense the massive energetic force behind you, somewhat out of focus to your mind, but crystal-lizing into perfect clarity of body, emotions, and mind, exactly where you are sitting now. If you don't sense it, then imagine it and your spirit-self will backfill your imagination with pictures, feelings, or just plain knowing (it does it all the time anyway). And please don't just believe this. Belief is sudden death to your search for the truth. Once you believe, you stop looking. If you're skeptical, good. Keep looking until you finally meet your true self. You are there, waiting for you.

But back to the question: "How come I don't know about this spirit-self that's supposed to be me?" This needs a little background.

A long time ago, before history as you perceive it, a number of nonphysical beings, each a vast entity in its own right, decided to colonize a planet to undertake some research on behalf of the Source. One of you volunteered to serve as the consciousness of the planet. The group helped this being to systematically densify its energy down through the dimensions. Meanwhile, the rest of you were conceiving the blueprints for the various life-forms that would occupy the planet, to be chemically encoded in what you call DNA. And by successive stepdowns in frequency over eons of time, the planetary consciousness burst through an energy barrier into the solid form you know today as planet Earth.

Over vast periods of your elapsed time, these beings continued to create lower-frequency projections of them-selves, still nowhere near physical yet. Slowly, these projections experimented with even lower frequency forms of themselves to produce what those with psychic vision would call fifth-dimensional and fourth-dimensional (astral) forms. Again slowly — over eons — you, as one of these beings, experimented further with DNA, directing energy to densify more into standing waves of energy to form semi-visible "light" bodies. Finally, in a brilliant act of creativity, you burst through the dimensional barrier to create the physical structures of subatomic particles, atoms, and molecules, within standing wave envelopes that you also conceived. You could still dissolve these forms at will and project different ones. So you played for immeasurable periods, at no time identifying with your increasingly physi-cal projections. You knew that these ethereal bodies were just energy fields that you created, and into which you radiated energy for the fun of it. As you pushed further, these projected forms became more visible (as you would use the term), but there was, as yet, no one consensus shape (you might appreciate the playful nature of the Source — always pushing to be creative and to know itself through what it can do).

In order to experiment further, you took a bold step: you projected your consciousness into these forms. This allowed you to interact with yourselves in wholly new ways, impossible at the higher frequencies where you knew only unity. You allowed your consciousness to reside in these ever densifying physical forms for longer periods of time. Consciousness now had two vantage points — fifth-dimensional and physical — and you were fully aware in each form of your selves in the other form, but there was no perception of separateness between them.

Now this big party of self-exploration was great fun. New types of energy fields were tried. For example, you established different fields in order to explore thoughts and emotions separately. And, most important, you gave your projections almost an autonomy, a freedom to be stand-alone entities in their own right. This split into two simultaneous vantage points was the crucial turning point in the story (by now, history had rolled on to just a few hundred thousand years ago). The consciousness in each of these autonomous forms was still fully aware of its spirit nature, and separateness was not even a conceivable thoughtform — the mental construct just did not exist. At this point, the planet was literally your biblical Garden of Eden. The concept of death was not even possible, because if you got bored with one physical form, you simply dematerialized it, rolled your consciousness back up into your fifth-dimensional frequency, and projected another form. Along the way, you switched from energy projection to a physical birth process and decided on a basic body shape for the species' rapidly densifying physical form. Your legends are full of ancient memories of some of the variety of shapes predating this standardization.

Over thousands of years, you, as Spirit, slowly became fascinated with the intensity of the sensations possible in these now physical forms, and your emotional and mental fields became more centered in the lower fields rather than the spirit field. The intensity and richness of emotional experience was totally enthralling, and the sensations that came from being in a dense form were very seductive. You know the story from here — the birth of the ego. You initially intended that the outer ego-self would act as the information gathering interface with the physical plane on behalf of your spirit-oriented self, which would continue to make decisions about what was real and what to do in the moment. As the experiment proceeded over the millennia, the outward-looking ego began to form its own ideas about reality, and to refer back to the inward-looking spirit-self less and less. The outer ego became stronger, and its identity began to shift from inner states to outer states of being. As a result of this shift, the ego began to color what it perceived and to judge it good or bad according to physical sensation. Thus the inward-looking self began to be fed "pre-digested" information.

The ego's emotional and mental sensitivity to the energy of the spirit field waned as the energy of the physical field became more the focal point. The once simultaneous dual vantage points became separate points of consciousness, and the lower-frequency, physically-oriented vantage point lost sight of the spiritual one. Over the next few millennia, the perceptive gap widened to the point that the lower vantage point began to either doubt the existence of the higher one or to project it outside of itself, as an external being. Thus you split your perception of who you were, and the concept of gods was created, as mankind could no longer relate to the vast, multi-dimensional beings as part of itself. The only way to reconcile with the inner voices, the impulses from Spirit, and the memory of being far more than a limited human being was to project your vast, powerful, and all-loving natures out onto beings that you, as a species, created for the purpose. You continued to receive messages and feel the love from your inner spirit-selves, but ascribed them as coming from your external gods.

To finally drive in the wedge between Spirit and personality, you conceived of a brilliant veil: shame. By building the vibration of shame into the very cells of your body, you finally achieved a complete sense of separation, and the

Spirit-being you once knew yourself to be became a phantom memory, easily dispelled by the harsh light of your new reality.

You then perceived of yourself as a personality, not even knowing that you were cut off from Spirit, because you'd forgotten about ever having been a unity. You externalized that vast, heroic part of yourself into a deity that you created. And the shame ensured that you saw yourself as unworthy in the eyes of this fabricated deity. So, over time, you became separate — isolated in a bag of skin, looking out at a universe you no longer understood, trapped in time and space, with death as the only way out. All you had to help you figure it out was a set of learned responses called a personality.

Please remember that you planned all of this from the beginning. You, as one of the group of beings that designed this experiment, had decided to see how far you could separate your perceptions from your nature — pure Spirit. Enormous ingenuity was required to design and create the veils that were to separate the dimensions, so that you would incarnate with no memory of who you really were. As part of this veiling, your collective spirit-functions made a decision that was to affect every incarnation for the next two hundred thousand years and completely alter the nature, purpose, and content of human life on this planet. You invented karma!

Karma

The basic thrust of the Source is to discover more about itself. *That is why everything anywhere exists!* The Source knows that its nature is one of complete harmony within itself — that is, it loves itself. To explore this love, it needs a vantage point outside itself. It needs to be able to stand apart, look at itself, and experience that love for itself. This is most effective if the part that is looking perceives itself to be separate from the whole and yet loves the whole as though it were not separate. You reasoned that the greatest joy would come when a part of yourself that perceived itself as separate would come to love the whole by its own volition. So you decided to continue with the emergence of separate vantage points even though you saw a potential risk for the species.

As a group, you tried an amazing experiment — something very bold, and certainly unique in the universe. You decided to erase all knowledge and feeling of your intimate oneness with the Source from your now autonomous projections. You decided that a veil would be drawn between consciousness and Spirit at birth, so that a newborn would forget its true nature. Thus the "you" reading this voluntarily subjected yourself to amnesia at birth. You erased all or most of the memory of your spirit nature at birth, to see if your ego-self would figure out its true nature during its physical plane life. Or would you leave the physical plane still in ignorance, to be surprised on rejoining your spirit-self? And how would you treat others of your own kind? Would you joyously revere the spirit evident in them and the planet, or would you feel so cut off from your own nature that you would deny the spirit in others? If so, would you see them as a threat and harm them?

You devised certain rules to guide these interactions within the game. Any exchange between two incarnees was to be balanced, either between them or between other incarnees of the same spirit-self, be it an act of kindness or cruelty. This balancing is what you have called the Law of Karma.

Please remember that the Source did not impose this aspect of the game on you, and no-one is "keeping score." You and your fellow co-creators added this little twist. Karma has got some bad press because of a little misunderstanding. The law that one act of cruelty must be compensated for by another is just a limited, third-dimensional interpretation of karma. Cruelty could just as easily be compensated for by a subsequent act of kindness or by forgiveness on the part of the so-called victim. You hoped that, through these clues, your incarnations would eventually figure out what was happening, come out of your amnesia, and get to the point of unconditional acceptance or love for the other amnesia suffers.

As an aside, remember that your spirit-selves operate in simultaneous time, so a karmic situation between X and Y in one lifetime could be balanced between Y and X in what you perceive as an earlier lifetime.

So the whole point of your adopting a karma-based system was to create intense emotional situations, to see how you (the physical plane ego-self aspects of yourselves) would respond. Would you kill, steal, and fight out of fear, or would you act out of love, to help, forgive, and acknowledge Spirit in others?

Of course, natal amnesia has to be total in most cases, but each lifetime holds the potential for awakening to your true nature. An unprompted realization of this nature — and the wave of unconditional love that automatically follows — allows you, the player in this cosmic game of hide-and-seek, to suddenly find the "hider" and realize that it was you all along.

The Law of Grace

What I've just described was the game until now. By common consent, your spirit-selves have decided that enough has been learned from karma. As the planet is on a "fast track" to ascension, we've got to wrap it up quickly. No more karmic imbalances can be created, and existing imbalances can either be scratched or played out, at your discretion. You may, therefore, see a dramatic rise in violence over the next few years, as you shake out the remaining imbalances.

I hope that you now see why your spirit-self has kept your ego-self in the dark. You did it deliberately to yourself, to give yourself the experience and opportunity to realize your true nature from all the clues lying around, to realize the true nature of others, and to see the Source in all things. To aid in this process, and to speed things up, you and the planetary consciousness have collectively requested that Grace Elohim bring its energy to Earth. This energy allows you to shake all this old energy out of your fields, and to break any old karmic agreements you have with other incarnations or your own and other spirit-selves across time.

The energy of Grace erases any and all karma, and in Part Two we will try some invocations for accelerating this process.

So, What About Darwin?

Much of this chapter flies in the face of the theory of evolution — man's emergence from the primeval ooze and all that. So what? That was a hundred years ago, and was only a hypothesis based on the flimsiest of evidence anyway. Paleontologists have tried to guess the big picture of the creation jigsaw from a few pieces of bone. The story of the origin of the species is not a linear, bottom-up progression, but a nonlinear, top-down densification. Your spirit-selves had better things to do than supervise things climbing out of the sea to develop lungs, arms, legs, and — finally — enough consciousness to relate to their creators. And if, as some believe, the species "grew" its own spirit-selves as it developed, why are you trying to get in touch with them again? There would be nothing to find.

And to cap it all, ask yourself whether it seems possible that something could crawl out of the ocean and develop a brilliant consciousness that could turn around and explore its own nature and origins. No, my friends, consciousness developed mankind, and not the other way around. You are Spirit-in-flesh. Rather than climbing up from the mud, you climbed down from Spirit. You densified beyond the point of awareness of Spirit, and have spent the last few thousand years trying to regain it. Spirit never forgot. The path back is still there, only now it's a high-speed elevator!

Sense the truth of this within yourself. Which feels more true to you? Evolving from a protein soup, somehow picking up consciousness along the way, and now telling yourself that there's more to life than being the descendant of a protozoan? Or starting as Spirit and taking part in an experiment to lower your frequency, knowing that, for the experiment to be realistic, you would have to forget your true nature as Spirit?

Suppose you were very rich, living in a big, fine house, and you wondered what it would be like to be, say, an Amazonian Indian. You could go on a field trip and live with a tribe, but you would know that you were just pretending. So, you undergo hypnosis to replace your memory with the memories of a tribe member. Now you live in total realism, unaware of yourself as anything other than a tribe member.

After a few years, a team of psychologists kidnap you, and restore your memory, and reinstate you in your fine house. Now you really know what life in the jungle is! You ate, slept, hunted, and lived with the tribe. You may have mated to produce a replica of your physical form. Out there in the jungle, you might have had faint memories of a different way of life, a life where getting dinner didn't require killing it before it killed you, somehow a little more civilized and beyond physical survival.

Well, thanks to your outer ego-self, you-as-spirit really knows what life on the physical plane is like! But you're on to the game now. If you're getting any faint memories of another way of being, or just the feeling that there's more to life that you're not getting, then you've awakened to the fact that you've been in the physical plane jungle all these years, hypnotized by the amazingly realistic scenery and props.

The movie "Total Recall" gives us an excellent model for this, in which a future civilization uses technology to implant an entire set of memories of, say, a vacation. After the treatment, you are sure that it all happened because you've got the memories. Think about your last vacation. Apart from the tan and some photos (which could have been rigged anyway), the vacation exists only in your memory. Couldn't you have just laid under a sunlamp and had the memories implanted in your brain? No. Of course, it was real ... wasn't it?

But how does knowing this help you get beyond an emotional and intellectual "Sure, I've got it. So?" How does it help you to open your fields up once more, to identify fully with, and embody, Spirit? That brings us to the game that replaces karma: divine expression, as it's been called.

5

Divine Expression:
The Field of Spirit

In the previous chapter, we talked about how you got you to where you are. Now let's look a little more closely. Everything is organized energy, and Spirit is no exception. The Source is aware, organized energy, on a scale that can't be imagined. In its continual playing of the game of knowing itself, it partitions itself. These partitions are analogous to vast thoughts (or plans for realities) that interact with themselves. They have no names or forms that you would recognize, yet they are aware of themselves as part of the Source and also aware of themselves as themselves.

Imagine lots of buckets of water suspended in water, and that all of the water is conscious. The water in the buckets knows that it is constantly exchanging with the water outside of the buckets, yet by virtue of its being contained, it is aware of itself as distinct from the water outside of the buckets. Of course, the buckets are imaginary, but they are analogous to the fields that support energy, and the water is analogous to the energy that fills them. Some fields are huge — like the planetary or solar fields — and others are tiny in comparison — like the field of an atom — but all of them contain and nurture the energy of the Source.

In addition to interacting with the fields, this conscious energy is also partitioned by another distinction: frequency. Think about a piano keyboard. All the individual notes are of the same basic stuff — vibrations on wires — but any note implies and contains all of its harmonics and subharmonics (the notes in the same relative positions in higher and lower octaves). In ways impossible to describe, the Source partitions itself into energy gestalts that know their unity, yet are aware of the other gestalts that make up the whole. Each gestalt creates subharmonics of itself, each of which is in turn aware of the subharmonics of the other gestalts. So Spirit of all frequencies knows itself to be the pure, joyful, creative energy of the Source.

By virtue of being, Spirit expresses the nature of the Source through the fields it generates and the energy that it radiates into them. Take, for example, Ariel. Some of you know this energy as an archangel. Ariel is the function responsible for projecting the field required for the physical plane — the field conducive to energy, which is necessary to support the energy as it bursts through into the material plane. At certain points in the field, conductivity is enhanced and the process is more efficient, resulting in physical matter as energy units congregate and coagulate. In less conductive parts of the field, they simply don't. And it is all by conscious agreement. So space is really a collective thoughtform that you all hold, but holding this thoughtform of space is just one of your many functions. And at any point in time, the energy performing this function is different from a moment ago. It has already changed while you've been reading this paragraph.

If you are called Mary Jones, the energy performing the Mary Jones function (or any function, for that matter) changes constantly. Now Mary's function may be to explore an aspect of motherhood, the use of power in relation to a child or sick parent, or any of a million things that Spirit wants to explore. Also, whatever the function is, the same theme may be repeated across many incarnations from a slightly different perspective in each one. So the Mary Jones function furthers the cause of the Source learning more about itself. Mary's personality and spirit-self collectively determine how close she comes to consciously realizing her true nature as a part of the Source and therefore experiencing her undividedness with everything and everyone around her.

So we look at the world of Spirit in two ways. Firstly, Spirit is pure organized energy, aware of itself and of its oneness. In this capacity, it doesn't do anything; it just is. Secondly, we see Spirit performing certain functions such as the Mary function, the John function, the St. Germain function, and of course, the Serapis function. The energy performing these functions changes all the time. The portion of Spirit performing the Serapis function, for example, is changing constantly, yet it understands the nature of the task and retains the appearance of consistency and continuity.

Functions vary in scope. The Serapis function is relatively well-defined and makes up a larger function charged with supporting the intellectual clarity needed for fully conscious ascension on a planet-wide scale. Different levels of Spirit perform different levels of this function in a well-orchestrated operation. For example, the channel "Tony" is the level of my function that gets these thoughtforms down on paper, and, at another level, I am putting this information out on the planetary group-mind grid, for all to tap into.

There is no one conductor in this orchestration, by the way. The units of consciousness serving Spirit just know what's going on and blend in at the appropriate level to literally "lend their energy."

Why this happens brings us to the title of this chapter. Spirit has an inexorable impulse to create, maintain, destroy, and create again, and seeks any and every opportunity to do so. Some levels of Spirit have a propensity for, say, intellectual creativity, while others prefer to clear away old belief systems to create the way for the new. Destruction is every bit as creative as creativity — it's just a matter of viewpoint.

Spirit seeks to express. The Source knows itself through its creativity. Your inner spirit-self seeks to express through your outer ego-self. You created the three lower energy fields of your body and personality to provide arenas for, and a means of, expression. You packed, and are constantly packing, energy into these arenas. You have put your ego-self into carefully designed situations with parents, school, and friends — situations that imprinted the ego with beliefs at an early age. You carefully selected the blend of energy that runs in your fields, and to some extent, you leave your ego-self to deal with them. But this does not mean that ego and spirit are in any way separate. You are your spirit-self as much as you are anything. You express it with every thought, word, and deed. When you act from love, you allow Spirit to flow through you unimpeded. When you act from fear (displaying hate, jealousy, greed, etc.), you are blocking the flow of love from Spirit. The only barrier between ego and Spirit is fear. Fear cuts ego off from Spirit, and as you, the ego-self, learn more about your true nature, the knowledge will begin to erode fear. As you let go of your fears, you allow yourself to become more emotionally and intellectually aware of Spirit, and that allows more love in. In this universe, the basic currency is the emotion of love. It will find any way in that it can. As it flows in, it dispels more fear, which allows even more love in, and so on.

So Spirit expresses through ego, the "I" that consciously knows itself. You, the ego-self, are the physical plane "leading edge" of your vaster spirit-self. You are its eyes, ears, and hands. Your ego-self deals with the events around you, deciding what to do about what, but you, as ego and Spirit, jointly decide what events shall come up. How do you know what to expect? What will the next hour bring?

To know these things, you would widen your conscious focus to include your spirit-self. I do not advocate removing focus from the physical plane entirely, because this would negate why you incarnated here. I do advocate, however, becoming fully aware of the contents of your three lower fields, as a prelude to coming to identify with Spirit and to embodying Spirit in your lower fields.

So the field of Spirit is one more field, over and above the three we've already talked about. You live within it, but because Spirit is not limited by space or time, it is not only around "you," as are the lower fields; this aspect of you is "everywhere." It empowers your other fields and expresses through them. You are not, therefore, just your personality or outer ego-awareness. You are much, much more. Part Two looks at how you can claim this larger identity and wake up to who you really are. But first, let's close Part One by taking a look at three areas of pervasive and troublesome myth that abound in the consensus reality: myths about love, truth, and power.

6

Three Great Myths:
Love, Truth, and Power

O ne of the drawbacks of denying your spiritual part is that you don't get to benefit from its larger point of view. As a result, distortions about everyday things can creep in, and have been doing so for millennia. Thus you may misunderstand some key aspects of your life. Living in ignorance has been appropriate in the past, because to have known more would have "blown the game" and invalidated a part of the experiment that you've set up on this planet. But now it's time to take the lid off, and I propose to address three great myths: love, truth, and power.

The Myth of Love

The great myth of love is that you can love someone, something, or even yourself. No one can love another! You cannot love yourself or anyone else! Why? Because love is not a "doing," but an *allowing*.

The very energy from which this universe is built is infused with a certain quality: a joy of being, an acceptance of the right of all things to be, and a delight in the expressions of all things as they enjoy their right to be. All beings are of the Source, and have a divine right to experience and express their divinity, and all beings have a right to enjoy the expressions of others, because all beings are really one, cleverly disguised to look separate.

Allowing this joy and delight in the expression of yourself and others is a wonderful experience, and is what I call "love." However, you cannot *do* joy or delight. You can only allow it to sweep through you, like any other emotion. And this emotion is not conditional on what any other beings are actually doing; it's based on knowing and experiencing the divinity in them. If someone you know is in a foul mood, for example, they're still expressing their divinity, even though that expression doesn't turn you on.

So, love is not something you do. It's a response in you to a particular frequency of energy flowing in, through, and around you constantly. Many things can deaden you to the relatively subtle energy of love. Fear, of course, will prevent you from sensing it, and will distort what little you do sense. Fear is not the opposite of love. It is the defensive gatekeeper, and simply will not allow you to sense the high frequencies in your fields. And the fear is locked in your belief system, or your *opinions* about reality, and has nothing to do with reality itself.

Love is allowing yourself to sense this energy as it relates to you, to others, and to the universe in general. It begins with acceptance of your right to be, and the right of others to be. This acceptance builds to an appreciation of yourself and others: of your qualities, gifts, and basic goodness. And it continues to build to a delight and fascination in self and others.

So, how do you allow this to happen? You begin by dropping the fears you have of being separate from Spirit, of being unable to cope with life, of being worse (or better) than other people. Once you see yourself and others as vast, multi-dimensional beings squeezed into tiny little bodies, these fears drop away. This isn't easy — you swim around in a thick soup of fear called the consensus reality all the time. But, as we'll see later, this is just people's opinion about what's real, and bears no resemblance to truth. Now (of course), you carefully built consensus reality over the millennia, and it has served the game of separation very well.

Because of the deep-seated fears that most folks carry around with them in their fields, they can't tell love from fear. So what you call love is actually a manipulative exchange of attention and affection. People who won't or can't love themselves (that is, they can't see or allow their own divinity) desperately search for someone else to make them feel secure, and when this security is threatened, they may fall back on emotional blackmail and control by withholding affection, all in the name of love.

Many times, when you hear one person say to another, "I love you," they really mean, "I am afraid and need you as my security blanket." Or one person in a relationship will have sex with a third person and the other person will say something like, "How could you? I thought you loved me!" What, I ask you, has seeing the divinity in someone got to do with exclusive rights to someone's body? What's really happening is that the angry partner feels insecure. If he or she could see the divinity in themself and their partner, the probable response would be, "Was it good?" But please see all this as perfect. Taking separation this far has required your utmost ingenuity, and it's been a stunning success.

Love is relaxing into your true nature. You can't really get hurt by opening up to this energy. Sure, other folks operating from fear may give you a hard time, but try to see their behavior as fear-based responses, not aimed at you, personally, but at what you *represent* to them. Thus they are acting from their own fears, and their behavior has nothing to do with you (this point of view is an essential component of becoming "transpersonal," but that's a whole other subject).

So, please see yourself as infinitely loved from the higher dimensions, especially by your spirit-self. Let go of the fear of being alone. You are not alone, nor ever could be. Come to accept yourself, appreciate yourself, and delight in who you are. Then you can begin to sense the love of Spirit as it flows through you. And remember, love need not be directed at anyone in particular; it's just the Source loving itself.

Once you allow yourself to sense this energy flowing through you, you'll find that the flow will increase, and it will inevitably flow from your fields to everyone around you, changing how you deal with them, and they with you. One day, the dam will break and you will find your fields flooded with unconditional acceptance for everyone and everything. Everything is made of "god-stuff," so what's not to love?

"Wait, a minute!" You might say, "I'm surrounded by mean-spirited people all day long. How can I love them?" Do not try to resist their personality quirks or they'll just get worse. Just open your heart chakra and sense the energy of love in your fields. If you open your heart chakra, other people will have to work hard to keep theirs closed. And thank them for giving you an opportunity to put this simple energy trick to work.

Hate, jealousy, and so on are simply signs of a fear-based personality which can't sense the energy of love within its fields. Give that person a jump start by channeling love at them. If their fear is too great, it may not work, but at least the outpouring from you keeps their fear from infecting your fields. Without being patronizing, have a little compassion for it, because feeling so cut off from Spirit is a scary place to be. Remember?

Never before in the history of this planet have the energies been more conducive to opening to this energy. Allow yourself to resonate with this new energy as it pours through your fields, and let it permeate all your relationships with everyone: lovers, friends, the mechanic who fixes your car, and the checkout clerk at the supermarket. You're Lightworkers coming on line before the rest of the population, and you've volunteered to start the ball rolling. So when you feel this resonance, you feel secure enough to allow your friendships to go to new levels of intimacy. Fear of intimacy is simply the fear of loss of identity, but I assure you that in such openness, you will find *more* of yourself, not less. When two people both allow themselves to resonate to the energy of love, free of conditional bargaining and future expectations, they begin to operate spirit-to-spirit. Within this full expression of who they are, it becomes easy and natural to share themselves mentally, emotionally, and physically. Sex, therefore, becomes the joining of spirit-in-flesh rather than being a commodity to be bartered for security or a good dinner. Your physical body is a glorious expression of Spirit, and sharing this expression with other people freely, openly, and joyfully is just one more aspect of your divinity.

And what if you're in a relationship that begins to die? The old way was to "work at it," in the hope of reconciling your differences and coming to some compromise. But now you know that your energetic signatures are no longer meshing. It's no one's fault, so make your peace and move on before you hurt each other. Hanging on to the grisly end serves no one, least of all Spirit. You had a spirit-to-spirit agreement to be together for a certain length of time, and your signatures were in resonance. But once the agreement's over, the resonance falls out and it's almost like you're strangers. Honor that and call it quits. And let go of the fear that there won't be another relationship, because that energy in your fields will drive off the next person through resonance. Instead, set up open anticipation in your fields, and stand back!

It may be difficult to see the perfection of the plan when your primary relationship has just ended, for example. It may bring up all kinds of stuff: abandonment, pain, shame, guilt, unworthiness, and so on. Where's the perfection in all that? Remember that you decided to participate in it for your own purposes. It may have been to break old patterns (like looking outside of yourself for approval), to bring new insights about the nature of love, or to move you into a transpersonal state. Whatever the reason, look for the big picture and ask how it serves you. You may have needed to be alone to go through some changes, or be free to begin a new relationship, or to move to another part of the country.

You are a Lightworker, here on a mission, and you've set up certain experiences to equip you to do your job better. This is not a random universe, and nothing happens without a larger purpose, so try to see the big picture. But above all, please don't think that anything was *done* to you. It's all right to feel a little victim energy for a while in order to clear it from your fields, but letting "victim" become part of your identity doesn't serve. That denies your mastery and gets in the way. And remember, also, that the Cosmic Joke is buried in there somewhere, if only you could remember the punch line!

The Myth of Truth

Another great myth of the physical plane is that there is something called "The Truth." This particular myth has been the cause of more wars and conflict than all the other myths put together. The notion that you could express multi-dimensional concepts in English, German, or any other current language is outrageous (although Hebrew comes a lot closer than any other).

No, my friends. On the physical plane, all you'll hear are *opinions*, often based in turn on the hand-me-down opinions of other people, picked up somewhere along the way. So treat everything you hear, see, and read as opinion, including the ideas in this book. There is only one person who can judge what is real and true for you: you!

If you believe that the world is a hostile place, ruled by an angry, vengeful god, then so it is — *for you*, that is. Or if you believe that the universe is benevolent and that Spirit is guiding you at each step, then that's what you'll experience.

Reality is infinitely complex and malleable because it's designed to be that way. The universe is not a static mechanism within which you have to find your way. It's created specifically to support *all* beings in an infinite variety of expressions of the Source. This creativity is how the Source knows itself and grows. And this includes supporting you in your expression of what you believe to be true. The folks at Earth Mission in Sedona, Arizona summed it up delightfully with "The Universe rearranges itself according to your pictures of reality." The universe is indeed a reality creation playground, and what you create — knowingly or unknowingly — depends on what you believe to be real (i.e. your pictures of reality).

Now, you store your opinions about reality in your fields. These are the "pictures" you hold about you, and you in relation to everything else: Spirit, other people, your job, your mate, and the universe in general. The events in your daily life are actually fabricated in a higher-dimensional, holographic-like framework — a kind of "reality factory." You, in collaboration with everyone you work with, play with, or just know casually, meet in this nonphysical reality factory to create the circumstances and events of your respective physical plane lives (you may catch yourself doing this while dreaming, for example).

Two main factors determine the kind of experiences that you'll bring into the physical plane. Obviously Spirit has an agenda. This is always positive and beneficial to your growth, even though it may not seem so, moment by moment (look hard enough and you'll see why you had that car wreck or had your purse stolen). As we approach ascension, you'll find that experiences intensify and the pace of life speeds up, because you're trying to crack open old pictures of reality and replace them with new ones at an ever-increasing rate.

The second major influence on the events you experience are your pictures of reality. Limiting, fear-based pictures make it difficult for Spirit to bring through healing, loving encounters with yourself and others. Someone living in fear is just not giving permission for Spirit to put through love-based experiences. This means, of course, that even love may be interpreted through the eyes of fear, and thus distorted.

If there is no one "galactic truth," this means that you can pick any set of truths you like to make up your pictures of reality. So it makes sense to pick those that bring you joy and allow you to be happy. But please don't think that you'd be living in a fool's paradise. You'd actually be living in a very sane person's paradise. But, even then, there's an alternative.

You could work very hard at trying to figure out what to believe is true (mankind has been hard at this since the days of separation, so you'd be in good company). But once you pick something to believe in, you automatically stop searching and exclude everything else that could be true. For example, limiting the Source to the Christian definition of God excludes the qualities of Allah, Yahweh, the Great Spirit, and the countless other deities described throughout time. Why not take the easy way out and ask yourself, as Spirit, what's true? Here you have all the answers you'll need, at least for the rest of your time on the physical plane.

Contacting yourself as Spirit has never been easier. Some folks dash from one channel to the next, desperately seeking "The Truth." And there's no shortage of people willing to be an outside authority. But you have all the answers within you, so stop, relax, listen, and trust. You may have a little trouble initially distinguishing between Spirit and an overactive mental body that wants to control the experience. Just thank it, and tell it to get out of the way so that it can learn some neat stuff. That usually works.

So there is no one "Reality" and no one "Truth." There are your pictures of reality that you inherited from your parents, teachers, and peers. And there is the viewpoint of

Spirit, as it flows through your fields (often distorted, however, by limiting pictures of reality). Because of such distortion, an encounter with Spirit is often attributed to contact with aliens, the devil, a god projected outside the self, or "just your imagination."

As never before, you-as-Spirit are trying to batter through the pictures of reality that you-as-personality are holding. Ascension is such a vast concept that these little pictures have to go if you are to grasp even a fraction of what it means. So let go of any opinions of who you think you are, who you think other people are, and what you think Spirit is. Keep your belief systems wide open and your discrimination alive and well.

If belief is certain death to understanding, what do you have left? *Belief* stems from wishing something to be true. It is built on preconceptions and prejudices, and opens its mind only to whatever fits its models. *Faith*, on the other hand, is a plunge into the unknown with an open mind, in the certain knowledge that it's all right to let go. Faith knows that it won't necessarily be safe or comfortable, but that it will be all right. Belief hangs on; faith lets go. You cannot find truth through belief, but only through the simplicity of faith.

Faith is the point of departure, but many searchers abandon faith along the way in favor of clutching at some belief or another. You cannot discover the mystery via beliefs, because you can only believe what you already know. But truth is beyond imagination. Nothing you can imagine could capture the enormity and glory of what's about to happen. So the only course is faith, an open mind, and an open heart.

The Myth of Power

When you look at the world today, you see examples of groups and nations using force to invade and attack other groups and nations. It may be to take natural resources like land or oil, to destroy a culture or belief system, or simply because DNA has given one group a different physical appearance. At the heart of the great myth of power is a deep-seated sense of separation and a resulting confusion about "power with" and "power over."

Power Over

When the world talks of a powerful man or a powerful woman, what exactly is the power?

If you define the world using only the five physical senses, then power is defined by what you can see, touch, feel, and hear. So you see power as dominance, or "power over" others, power over the environment, and even power over self. And because of the way societies define power, and focus it in a few individuals, societies must set up organizations to prevent its misuse. So you have watchdogs who scrutinize the power holders.

When a society or group defines power in terms of the ability to direct the use of resources (such as money, human lives, armies, weapons, food, and raw materials), the greatest fear is the loss of that power to someone else or some other group. And power over others reinforces and deepens separation because you can't exercise power over others without making them "other," be it based on religion, ideology, skin color, or gender.

When personality looks outside of itself for power, it turns to material things and other personalities. This leads to a pecking order of "more powerful than me" and "less powerful than me." There is an alternative to this false kind of power, however. As we'll see, turning to Spirit reveals a power based on creativity, loving cooperation, reverence, harmony, and heroic collaboration.

Power With

This alternative power is based on power "with"— with Spirit and with your fellow humans — and ironically the first step to "power with" is surrender. But surrender to Spirit sounds like acquiescing to something that has power over you, and isn't that just the same old story but with a different overlord?

"Power over" requires the submission of one to another, in which both feel separate. "Power over" works only when this sense of separation exists. To the extent that you feel separated from Spirit, surrender will feel like submitting to a superior force, like a besieged city finally opening its doors to looting and rape by a conquering army. If, on the other hand, you sense a seamless unity with Spirit, surrender simply means enlarging a small, fear-based agenda to the much vaster agenda of planetary and personal ascension — replacing "I've got to do it all by myself" individualism by alignment with the unimaginably powerful forces at work on planet Earth today.

The problem with power based on *who* you are as a personality, separate from Spirit, is that you can lose it. Other people can steal your resources, age can steal your strength, and illness can steal your health. But power based on *what* you are cannot be stolen. Seeing yourself as a vast, multi-dimensional being having a human experience, rather than a human having a spiritual experience, puts you in touch with your true power and its unlimited creativity and potential.

Ironically the single most powerful thing that any of you have ever done was to become human, and that didn't actually require you to *do* anything. You grew your body in the womb; at birth or just before, you embodied a part of your identity in that tiny form, and then drew the veil in order to forget what you'd done! That is one of the most powerful acts done anywhere in any universe, because you said, "I am strong enough and vast enough to carry out this lifetime. I can blindfold myself to my own vast being and succeed among billions of others who have done the same thing. We might fight and bicker, but we'll pull it off and come to remember."

So you forgot your true power along with your true identity, all to make the game more realistic. When you are unaware of your true power, you have to scramble to grab what you can before anyone else. Every unkind or harmful act committed on this planet has been done by someone who felt powerless in some way, and the stronger the feeling of powerlessness, the greater the unkindness or harm in the act.

You can only exercise power over others if you have a picture of reality that says that they're separate from you. You can change your pictures of reality around "separation," but what makes coming to true power more difficult is the fact that you carefully built a cornerstone of separation into the human race at the cellular level. Very few people actually feel true unity at a deep physical level. In fact, most people feel something quite different — shame — and that's held at the cellular level.

Shame

Personality initially served as the "eyes and ears" for Spirit on this planet, but eons ago, when you decided to experience a game of separation, personality assumed an identity separate from Spirit, and you formed an outer ego to take on the role of Spirit in determining what's real and what to do about it. To keep outer ego unaware of the fact of separation from Spirit (the so-called "fall of man"), you laid a very particular energy into the species' genetic structure. This vibration feels slightly different to each person: some feel like "fallen angels," others feel as though it's only a matter of time before they're caught for some nameless offense, and others feel somehow dirty and soiled. And folks will go to great lengths to avoid these feelings of unworthiness. Try looking at some of the events of your life from this perspective. See what I mean?

Compensating for the shame shows up in many different ways: in elitism or competition, for example. When you feel separate from each other, and don't even know for sure that there is something called Spirit, it's inevitable that outer ego will seek safety in trying to get higher up the ladder than other people. The reason that TV news focuses on death, doom, and disaster is to allow people to feel that someone somewhere is having a worse time than they are, and that they are temporarily a little more safe because it didn't happen to them today. Feeling cut off from Spirit, the personality views life almost as a punishment, rather than as a gift and an opportunity for expression, which gives new meaning to the term "life sentence."

The important thing about this shame is to know that you inherited it in your genes. On planet Earth, it just comes with the territory, but shame is so deeply a part of having a physical body that it never gets examined for what it is: a condition of being incarnate. And every time anyone says something like, "You should be ashamed of yourself," the knife turns in the wound, because at a very deep level, you agree with it.

Of course, you all set the game of separation up this way. You couldn't just *pretend* to be separate from Spirit. You had to make it realistic in order for the game to work, and you have found that shame works very well indeed! Shame lies at the center of every cell of your physical body. Normally at death, you can leave this shame behind in the cells, but in order to ascend *with* the body, this energy must be released from your cells.

Cellular Release

Many Lightworkers are blazing a trail for the rest of the population to do this. In extreme cases, they may find that they're suddenly forced into a position of powerlessness. This may cause a fast and massive release of shame from their cells into their fields where it can be cleared.

Not everyone will opt to do this, and most folks will choose a gentler, longer release. Either way, it's good to know that, when you feel shame of any kind, it's not "you," but just another energy to be released from your fields. Try not to allow the shame to be a part of your identity or feel guilty for being you. As Lightworkers, you are transmuting the species' inbuilt shame to a higher expression of unity with, and service to, Spirit.

Under the guidance of Spirit, the energy of shame is being released from your cells into your fields. And as it comes up, you get to feel it as a foreground experience, rather than as an underlying condition of being human. And the way to deal with this is to go through it. Avoiding it or suppressing it is telling yourself that it's true, and that you're powerless to do anything about it. Simply look at shame as something inherited in the cells and from cultural imprinting, and *not* as your identity.

As you're burning the released cellular shame out of your fields, you will be feeling it. Allow this to happen, knowing that it's not "you," but something you came to this planet to deal with. If you feel alone and powerless, try to find a group of other Lightworkers, some of whom will also be doing this process. Don't be afraid to accept their help. The days of the rugged individualist are over. We have moved into an era of co-creation, and it's important to let it happen. Lightworkers are on assignment to this planet, but until now, you may have just been working solo. But you're now being called on-line, to work together with other Lightworkers to co-create the next level in the evolution of the species, as old separation-based patterns are being pulled out of the species' genetic heritage. You can't do this alone.

Another way to support yourself when shame comes up is to sense your true power. Ask Spirit for "ever-increasing capacity to do whatever it takes." Secondly, call on Destroyer Force angels to spin the energy out of your fields, and on St. Germain to "violet flame" your fields. After a few seconds or minutes, you'll feel calmer and subtly more powerful. Let this new sense of power flow through your body, and visualize it filling the void in your cells left by the released shame.

Control

Another part of the myth of power is the illusion of control. Any control you think you have over your life belongs to Spirit. When things work out, it's your spirit-self working through your fields. And when things don't work out, it's still your spirit-self working through your fields, but this time trying to get your personality's conscious attention or to bring something to personality's awareness. If things aren't going according to your plan, examine your pictures of reality, looking for signs of limitation and control. Trying to control and manipulate events according to personality's ideas of how things should be is a fruitless activity, and may lead to disappointment, frustration, and anger. So what can you do?

When you align with the intent of Spirit as it goes about its functions, you become an unstoppable force because you are going with the flow of the Universe. But this raises the old question, "How do I know the intent of Spirit?" One answer is, "Whatever makes your heart sing." Ariel offers this three-part test for deciding what to do: "Does it bring you joy? Is it fun? Does it serve the Light?" If all three are true, then you're following Spirit. If one or two are not true, then that course of action might not be aligned with Spirit.

If you ask these questions of your job, say, and get "No" to all three, then think seriously about changing jobs (or even careers), because you're not tapping into your true power. Going against the flow is hard work but going *with* the flow is relatively effortless and a lot more fun. Things fall together instead of apart, and people pop into your life to help rather than hinder.

So control is an illusion; the flow of Spirit is the reality. All that you are and all that you have is the result of your spirit-self setting things up. What you can do at the personality level is be conscious of this and add your input on the "reality factory" shop floor. You will be heard!

True Power

On the surface, shame and lack of control appear to have little to do with power. But they are linked because amassing control and power over others is a direct response to cellular level shame and an attempt to suppress it. You put the shame there to prevent you from sensing your true power. Therefore, true power is both the means of dealing with the shame, and the end result of releasing it.

True power is a "being" state, not a "doing" state. *Doing* power is the old way; *being power* is expressing Spirit. Now that doesn't mean sitting on a mat radiating energy for the rest of your life. You can still act, only now you're coming from that still, quiet place within you that knows that it's a vast, unlimited force working in harmony with All That Is.

Just as "the Tao that can be spoken is not the Tao," power that must act is not true power. True power is strong and yet humble because it knows its strength. Strength means walking without fear because to fear anything denies your ability to create your own reality. You walk in safety because there are no strangers and because you're in harmony with Nature and all her creatures.

In true power, you love freely because you do not fear rejection or pain. You give of yourself because you know that rejection is a sign of the other's inability to receive what you are. You do not compete with another because competition implies shame and denies the mastery of both of you. And you know that ultimately you're competing with yourself. True power cooperates selflessly, knowing that it can't be taken advantage of. It forgives unconditionally because you flow effortlessly through life and because you acknowledge your role in co-creating every event in your life. You blame no one, not even yourself, because you are following Spirit in every moment. You do not judge anyone or anything because you know that judgement is based on shame. Instead you look to Spirit for what is true in the moment. And from this perspective, you see everything as Spirit-in-expression, working through personalities. You may not see the perfection of the expression of others, but you know that you're not their judge, so you just give them the room they need without becoming embroiled in their expression.

If suffering comes into your life, you do not avoid it, but experience it and honor your creativity for having manifested it.

The greatest hallmark of the truly powerful person is the ability to share himself or herself with others, to let the love of Spirit flow unimpeded to others. As we've seen, love is not something you do but something you allow. And love only happens when you also allow your own power. I see many Lightworkers hiding behind a false humility or modesty, as they try to manipulate themselves into being "nicely nice." Please do not talk yourself out of your power. Many think that the cost of belonging to the so-called New Age movement is the abandonment of all power, including true power. They couldn't be more wrong. From the first aggressive thrust into the physical plane at birth, you are here to serve the planet and her indigenous population. You can't do that whimpering in a corner. You are Spirit-in-flesh and you came here with a mission. So let your true power out and *be* who you really are. Any actions you care to take will then be based on your true power, and in the "being" state of your vast magnificence.

This doesn't mean "No more Mr. Nice Guy," although it sometimes might. It does mean that if you do act, it will be from love, compassion, and fearlessness, and you will do whatever feels right in the moment. Sometimes you will act alone, and at other times you will co-create with other masters in their power. You are entering a time of glorious expression, and no part of you is unworthy of that expression.

I salute you for undertaking this lifetime and close this chapter by reminding you of just how powerful a being you really are, and that — in concert with other Lightworkers — you can co-create miracles.

Part Two ═══════════════════════════════

Ascension: How To Do It

art One covered what you might need to know as
preparation for ascension. We've seen how the human
species made its monumental decision to draw the
veils of amnesia at birth, so that you begin each incarnation
not knowing who you really are. Since mankind made that
decision, the race has expended enormous amounts of
energy in trying to solve the riddle, while still in physical
bodies and behind the veils. Mankind has postulated Spirit
as external to itself and called it God, or, sensing the vastness of Spirit, postulated a whole pantheon of gods to be
worshipped. Man has killed man because of disagreements
over concepts which they both invented. But in this glorious
experiment, the Source — you in the widest sense — learns
more about itself.

But now the experiment is over. It's time to pack up the
tents and move on: that's ascension! The most pressing task
now is for all the ego-self projections to consciously choose
to embody Spirit. That means aligning the three lower
energy-bodies with the energy of Spirit, and allowing Spirit
to flow freely through them, consciously. You, as Spirit, have
always worked through you as ego, but ego has been too
preoccupied to notice.

We are talking here about a deep knowing that you are
primarily Spirit in nature, rather than a body with feelings;
that you create your reality through your thoughts; that
everything you see around you is simply captured energy,
giving you the perception of solidity.

We are talking about the level of conscious awareness of
Spirit such that when you look at someone else, you know

without doubt that you and they are Spirit, made of the same stuff as the Source. We are talking about levels of knowing and unconditional love not known on this planet for hundreds of thousands of years, about the ability to consciously create any object or circumstance you wish, and about the unconditional love that this degree of power requires.

In Part Two, we look at what you can do to bring this about. The ironic thing about ascension is that it must begin with descension — the descension of Spirit into the physical, emotional, and mental fields. You, as Spirit, are responsible for this process, and we'll see what you can do to get your personality out of the way. You must be consciously aware of what's going on and want it to happen, of course. But once you at the ego level have built one half of the bridge, Spirit will build the other half and they'll meet in the middle. Your conscious role is to clean out your lower fields, get them aligned, and prepare them to handle the massive influx of high-frequency Light energy. Spirit's role is to flood these fields with your own energy and complete their alignment. Everything is Spirit, of course. It's just a matter of how much distortion your ego-self imposes when it expresses Spirit.

I offer steps and guidance for this process. However, be aware that the process differs for each person, so the guidance can only be general. Fortunately, as the channels between ego-self and spirit-self open more and more, Spirit will take over the guiding (it has done this before, many times). This personal guidance is far more valuable than anything you could receive from me or any outside authority. But the trick is trusting. Human nature puts more credibility on what comes in from outside. Learning to trust Spirit, rather than outside authorities, is a major part of the process.

Do you remember the space jello we talked about earlier — the fate of the yellow jello when a standing wave was introduced into the red jello, and how it would slowly build up the exact same standing wave? And how, if the yellow jello was totally enclosed in the red jello, the yellow would vibrate as one with the red? Being physical on the physical plane means that you are totally enclosed in a planet-wide field. Your fields not only interact with those of other people, picking up their energy and forming your own standing waves, but they are also totally immersed in every planet-wide field. If your fields are at all predisposed to the energy in another's fields, or in the planetary fields of the consensus reality, resonant standing waves are inevitable. And some of them are not very pleasant.

So, two things need to happen. First, you need to reduce your predisposition to any standing waves you don't want, and second, increase your predisposition to those that you do want. We'll look at both issues. First, we'll examine ways of disconnecting from dysfunctional energy in other people and the consensus reality by removing any dysfunctional energy of your own, and by raising the lowest frequency that your fields can hold to a frequency above the level where unwanted resonance can occur. Second, we'll examine ways of resonating with energy you do want in your fields — the energy of Spirit.

Remember that you, as Spirit, want you, as ego, to ascend more than anything else. In this sense, ascension for the ego involves its redefining itself as Spirit. This means looking, feeling, thinking, and being as Spirit. Ego doesn't have to change what it is, but only what it thinks it is. It has always been Spirit but didn't know it. This not knowing often distorted Spirit as it expressed through the ego. Now it is time to expand its awareness, drop the veils and fears, and embody Spirit. It's a culmination of an entire cycle of lives: "you" are the embodiment of your spirit-self that's going to lead every other incarnation across time into the Light. Until a few years ago, this process was extremely difficult. Raising your frequency and moving between planes required dedication and extensive training. But now the brakes are off. For example, an "elevator" has been created through the plane system. It was conceived by Sananda and we call it the Unity Band or Frequency.

Now, the planet is ascending anyway, so a major push is underway to get as many of you as possible to ascend along with the planet. In this part of the book, we see how.

7

Resonance 1:
Breaking Old Patterns

Resonance happens when one field responds sympa-
thetically to another field and energy is exchanged.
Imagine two identically tuned guitar strings side by
side. Pluck one to set up a standing wave and the other will
vibrate at exactly the same frequency. Similarly, put one
angry person in a room with other people and soon many of
them will feel angry. This is because their energy fields
contain anger which can resonate with the anger in others,
even though they're not feeling angry at the moment.

Anger is just an energy, and over the course of a few
minutes, the emotional body of everyone in the room
detects the energy that our angry friend transmits on this
frequency. Some people register it and begin to resonate in
sympathy with it because their fields also contain their own
anger energy of the same or similar frequency. To one degree or another, these folks unknowingly begin to build up a
standing wave of anger in their fields and suddenly find
themselves furious. They are simply resonating with the
energy of our friend who started the whole thing, but they
have no idea why the party suddenly turned sour for them.

Well, you know what's going on. What do you do about
it? Fortunately, knowing about field resonance provides
several techniques that you can use, both to change how
energy in your fields resonates with individuals and with the
consensus reality, and to regain control over the energy in
your fields.

The Unified Chakra

We are grateful to Ariel and Qu'an Yin for introducing the
information about the unified chakra to the planet. The shift

to the unified chakra is the most vital shift you can make because it consciously affirms a recent change in the way the species operates its energy bodies. Traditionally, the chakras were cone-shaped and centered at seven locations in the physical body field. They were the means by which your various energy fields exchanged energy. However, they are evolving from separate cones into one unified chakra centered on the heart chakra. This is important because a unified chakra allows you then to align your physical, emotional, mental, and spiritual bodies, and to harmonize their energy.

When you as Spirit were densifying and creating the main chakra system, you introduced an energy barrier to isolate the heart or fourth chakra from the other chakras. This was necessary for the karma game to work; it allowed the lower three chakras to run amok with little or no moderation from the heart chakra. Thus the heart chakra had little or no role to play in the interaction between the three basic energy fields. As a result, the major responses to life's situations were unbalanced and out of harmony: intellectual responses from the sixth chakra, empty communication and judgement from the fifth, ego and power-based responses from the third, sexual and creative from the second, and survival and fear-based responses from the first chakra. These responses were perfect for creating karma because the more balanced responses such as love and compassion were dampened.

Working with the unified chakra, you unify the higher and the seven lower chakras into one so that they all function in accordance with the frequency of love-based energy flowing through the heart center. This also means that your three lower energy fields can align with each other and exchange energy and resonate with each other, with love as the major component of the interactions.

By expanding the unified chakra outside of the physical body as well as within it, your physical body senses itself not just as a fleshy standing wave, but as the complex energy field it really is, in which some of its energy just happens to be visible. The mental and emotional fields are also energy, of course, but not as visible to most people. Next, all three fields can align quite easily into one unified field because at last they've found a set of frequencies which they can all understand: love.

The unified chakra eliminates all the processing that you've been used to and allows fast and easy alignment and unification of your energy bodies. Another major benefit is that you can now bring much more energy through the unified chakra into your unified field. You used to bring energy in (or channel) through separate chakras into separate fields and therefore emphasized, say, an intellectual or a power aspect of the channeled energy. Now you can bring in a wider spectrum of energy, especially its higher frequency love-based aspects. Also, when you channeled or did energy healing work, you may have felt a "buzz" as the energy hit resistances in your fields. You no longer feel this because your unified fields and chakras present no resistance to the energy. This also means that you act appropriately at all times. You now automatically and naturally blend just the right amounts of, say, love and sexual energy, or love and power energy for the situation. With a unified chakra, you don't need to worry about whether you are being appropriate. You know that you are.

Finally and most important, the unified chakra allows you to embody even more of your spirit-self. You are no longer trying to filter its love through your mental field or its higher wisdom through your emotional field. Everything you need comes through the unified chakra into the unified field at the same time and in exactly the proportions needed.

It is recommended that you unify your chakras several times a day. With a little practice, you'll be able to say, "Unify" to yourself, and instantly snap your chakras to one unified chakra. With Ariel's permission, we reproduce the full process in the appendix to this book.

Basically, the process involves getting into a comfortable, relaxed position, deepening your breathing, and breathing Light into the heart chakra. On each out-breath, you visualize your heart chakra becoming larger, opening in all directions like a sphere. You expand it to include each succeeding pair of chakras as you breathe in and out: third and fifth, second and sixth, first and seventh, *omega* and *alpha** (see Note, bottom of next page), eighth and your knees, ninth and your ankles, and the tenth and your feet. Your unified chakra is now a sphere of golden light, about twenty to fifty feet in diameter, and forms the center of your unified field, which could be several miles in diameter. Your spirit field coexists with this unified field. So now you ask the appropriate level of your own spirit to blend its energy with that of your unified field, starting at the center of the unified chakra.

You can go further and experience yourself as a truly multi-dimensional being by expanding your unified chakra to include the eleventh chakra (your group soul level), the twelfth chakra (the Christed level of your spirit-self), the thirteenth chakra (the I AM Presence), and the fourteenth chakra (the Source).

The unified chakra prevents the traditional focus of the separate chakra system that was so selective of the energy it handled. If you perceived anger or power being directed at you, you responded unconsciously with, say, the first chakra (fear), or with the third (power). So you either fled or stood your ground. A whole new pattern occurs with the unified chakra. You respond from your entire being, including Spirit, so you'll throw a heavy dose of love into the energy stew. You may say and do the same things as at the ego level, but the other person's fields will get the love energy and be somewhat confused initially. They attacked you, yet they feel this warm glow inside. In the confusion, one or both of you will smile and suddenly the tension is broken. So the unified chakra is the perfect panacea for all that ails you. But what about using it for constructive ends rather than just warding off destruction?

Well, although Spirit energy is high-frequency, it generates standing waves of energy with frequencies that are sub-harmonics of its own energy. These fit right into the

---

* NOTE: The alpha and omega chakras have been latent until recently, but have now been activated. The omega chakra (eight inches below the spine) connects you to the planetary consciousness and you should now ground from the omega rather than the base chakra. The alpha chakra (eight inches above your head) connects you to your fifth-dimensional Lightbody.

frequency bands of your physical, emotional, and mental fields. Working with separate chakras used to filter out some of this energy. The third, say, would handle power frequencies, and the fifth/sixth would handle thoughtforms, but no chakra could handle it all. So, depending on which chakras were open, you would only allow certain facets of your spirit-self into your lower fields. The unified chakra allows it all in — the entire spectrum of your being.

Your response comes from your whole being, meaning that you are active rather than reactive, love-based rather than fear-based, and transpersonal rather than personality-based. And now you will find that even anger is divine expression.

Unplugging From The Consensus

Another technique actually breaks off resonance with other people's transmissions and establishes new resonances with your spirit-self. You are part of the vast collective planetary consciousness and you not only derive energy from it but add your own energy to it, simply by being present in it. Adding your energy to any particular frequency of the countless frequencies that make up the conscious energetic gridwork of this planet increases the energy of that frequency.

Now some of these frequencies are not fun to tap into. For instance, if you are worried about money, you are resonating with planet-wide scarcity energy, adding to it and drawing from it simultaneously. Thus you put your mental and/or emotional energy bodies into resonance with everyone else's scarcity.

As the vibratory rate of the planet and of your energy bodies increase, any fear-based frequency will begin to feel increasingly uncomfortable. Also, as you increase your abilities to manifest your reality from your field, you will find that whatever energy you run will show up in your life more quickly.

So, how do you unplug from the fear-based frequencies of personality, and plug into the love-based frequencies of Spirit? Imagine an old fashioned telephone switchboard with all those wires going everywhere. These wires can plug into any of the holes on your switchboard. Now imagine that all the lower holes on the switchboard panel are where you plug into the consensus reality: fears, beliefs, habits, or anything that is not fun or joyful. The upper holes on the switchboard are "Joy," "Laughter," "Abundance," "Being in the Now," "Creativity," "Divine Expression," or anything else that is joyful, fun, and in Spirit. See yourself unplugging all the wires from the lower holes and plugging them into the upper row of Spirit.

If you are not in Spirit, you are simply channeling the energy of one or more unpleasant frequencies of the consensus reality, and you can choose who or what you channel. Simply choose to channel the energy of (and the reality held by) Spirit, as you embody it. Do this whenever you think or feel yourself to be anything other than a vast, multi-dimensional being, because the chances are that the feeling of limitation comes from being plugged into the lower, fear-based part of the switchboard.

The consensus reality is very seductive. You've been plugged into it all your life. You know it well and it holds no surprises. You know with certainty that "Shit happens," and breathe a sigh of relief when it happens to the other guy first. Notice how many freeway slow-downs are caused not by the actual accidents but by the rubberneckers wondering how bad it was.

Of course, others have a vested interest in keeping you locked into their reality. However, you will meet more and more people who are building an alternate consensus reality, one based on joy and love rather than on fear-avoidance as the determinant of how good or bad something is. It's all around you as a new set of energies with much higher frequencies. It's there for the taking. But you have to give something up: empathic and telepathic contact with those who wallow in fear-based energy. Their energy will try to resonate in your fields, quite impartially; that's the way energy works.

There are many reasons why your fields are inclined to resonate with the *status quo* consensus. First, you were born into it. As an infant with fields which were clear except for what your spirit-self put into them (note how babies are always in Spirit, even when they are crying), you were a sponge, ready to soak up whatever came along. And you did — by the bucketful!

You may have picked up some or all of the following imprinting: "I've got to work hard to make my way in the world," "Male breadwinner/female dependent," "Love is capricious, so don't fall for it," "If you're not first, you're nowhere," and "It's too good to be true."

The list is endless — a mixture of outmoded thought-forms and emotions, all taking you out of the Now-point into what might happen in the future. As a child, you picked them up from your parents, relatives, schools, and friends who had also been infected.

Anytime you're in someone's field who is transmitting on any frequency with which you might resonate, you pick up and amplify their stuff, feed it back to them, receive yet a higher dose back, and so on, all without your conscious awareness — positive feedback, like the output from a loud-speaker feeding back into the microphone. If this feedback serves you, allow it to happen, but if it feels "icky," it can ruin a beautiful day, and you didn't do anything to make it happen except to live in the planetary field.

So you need to purge all this stuff because it stops you from tuning into your favorite station: Spirit. How do you do it?

Listen and be fully conscious of what others are saying, thinking, and feeling, and most important, how it affects you. Purge your fields whenever you think of it — it's only energy, after all. Breathe it out of your fields by intent, or spin your fields.

When you see street-people, can you see them as glorious projections of Spirit? Does any thought or emotion come up which smacks of judgement, i.e. "better than", or "worse than," or "not me"? You may not like another person, but can you respect Spirit in them, no matter how well hidden? Can you accept any errant behavior as perfect for them? Do you recoil from someone with a disfigured face? Do you feel better than a homeless vagrant who reeks of cheap drink? If so, you've still got a little imprinting to pull out. But don't feel that you've failed some test of spirituality. It's only stuff. Just look at it, love it, and let it go. It has served you well all these years, but you don't need it anymore.

How about the circumstances of your life? Do you accept personal responsibility for everything you don't like: the car accident, getting laid off from work, the leaky roof, the row with your mate, or the lack of a mate? You create every minute event from one level or another of your being, and the contents of your mental and emotional bodies plays a very large part, whether you know it or not. There are no random elements in the universe. At some level, be it Spirit or personality, you create every second of your life. If the universe didn't work like that, it would mean either that people could put their stuff in your fields without your permission, or that things were happening to you that weren't in resonance with your field. Let me assure you that the universe doesn't work like that.

Now I'm not saying that you consciously want everything that's in your life, but just that you brought it in and put it there, so some part of you wanted it at some time. Maybe you took on imprinting that said that life's a hard taskmaster. If so, you would have a series of demanding jobs in order to prove yourself right, and that may have been appropriate at some point in your life. You create your own reality because the universe faithfully rearranges itself in order to manifest your blueprints. Your life is a perfect mirror of the blueprints you created from your beliefs. The reality you experience today reflects your reality picture. If you stop and think about it, it has to be that way — otherwise the universe would be random.

The people around you are part of your hologram and also reflect your pictures of reality back at you. If you didn't resonate with another person in some way, there would be no basis for a relationship, be it attraction or repulsion. This is how it works. Each time something significant happens in your life, you store the memory of it and the emotions you felt as high-frequency geometrical shapes (tetrahedrons, actually) in your mental, emotional, and physical fields. This energy can reinforce energy you are already holding there. So if your picture of reality is that you're a worthless little human being and someone is unkind to you, you let that opinion in and it reinforces your picture, mentally and emotionally. Worse still is that fear energy tends not to move, but stays stuck in your fields. On the other hand, if your self-image is positive, you know that the other person is reacting not to you but to something you represent to them. Something you did or said, or something about how you look, may remind them of something else entirely, which has nothing to do with you. So the negative energy of the encounter sits in your field as just a memory, with no emotional charge on it.

If two people meet and they both hold similar pictures of reality, their geometric shapes can interact and mesh (like attracts like). Thus, if a man and woman both believe that men are powerful and women are powerless, their geometries will click, mesh, and stick together. These people are now locked in a "sticky" relationship. On the other hand, if two people who believe in their own mastery meet, their geometries will also mesh. They won't get stuck, however, because their belief systems are open, their geometries are spinning much faster, and energy is constantly flowing in and out of their fields.

So, what do you like and dislike about your body, your emotions, thoughts, life circumstances, and friends? Is there anything you would change? Whatever you don't like tells you something about energy in your field. Otherwise, you wouldn't have noticed it. The energy would have just passed through unnoticed. Instead it hit some stuck energy, reinforced it, and you noticed it. You put it there for a reason, but do you still need it? If not, declare that you're a master in your own house and banish it like this, saying:

"I am a master of divine expression. I acknowledge that I feel _____ and that it no longer serves my path to Light. By the force of Grace, I release the energy of _____ back to the universe for the greatest good, to be transmuted into the highest form of Light."

Systematically dump all the old baggage you've collected over the years. You don't need it where you're going, and it will slow you down. We've already dealt with shame, but another particularly heavy set of baggage is *blame*. It's old energy and you can clear it as follows:

One at a time, visualize everyone with whom you've ever had significant dealings in your life: parents, mate, children, boss, landlord, and so on (calling up a vision of them puts you in touch with their spirit-selves). Tell them (internally or out loud, if you like) that you forgive them for any harm that you ever felt that they did to you (it doesn't matter if they don't think that they hurt you — it's what *you* think that's trapped in your fields). Tell them that you understand that it was all done by prior agreement, even if you didn't know that at the time. Thank them for fulfilling their end of the agreement, and tell them that you love them. (This process alone could take several hours.)

Next, stand in front of a mirror and do the same for yourself. Forgive yourself for every time you thought that you'd screwed up. Tell yourself that it was all done by agreement, and look at what you learned. Remind yourself that Masters never screw up — everything happens exactly as they intend it to. The only thing Masters need to do is serve the Light.

We're getting down through it by now. We've blown out imprinting, judgement, fear, and best of all, self-judgement. What's left? Maybe some stuff from your co-incarnees. Repeat the forgiveness routine, but this time more generally:

"I forgive anyone I think has harmed me in this or any lifetime, anywhere, on any plane. I forgive all debts and erase all karma. I choose Light for myself and for all my selves."

(Say this with meaning and intent. It may take a few tries but you'll know when it's complete.)

You can't manipulate yourself into forgiving yourself or others, however. Neither should you try, just because it's the "spiritual thing to do." To know if you have truly forgiven, look for gratitude. Once you feel gratitude for the imprinting or experience (even if it's major, like incest or rape), then you are free. You feel a deep, soul-level appreciation for yourself and the other person for serving you in such a challenging way. Such service requires great love and compassion. And remember, there are no victims — only co-creators. You designed the nature of your imprints and requested others to join in your game.

When you incarnated, you built several blocks and vows into your personality and energy bodies to prevent you from knowing who you really were. At the discretion of your spirit-self, it may be time to release these blocks and vows, not only for yourself but for all your bloodline back to the dawn of history (because this technique is so powerful, and affects every one of your ancestors, we had to obtain special dispensation from the various councils to release this infor-mation). *If it feels right for you*, either alone or in a group (group work is *far* more potent than solitary work), say the following with intent:

"I now rescind any and all vows that I have taken to experience the illusion of unconsciousness.

"As Lightbearer of my genetic lineage, I break these vows for myself and all of my ancestors.

"I declare these vows null and void in this incarnation, and all of our incarnations across time and space, parallel realities, parallel universes, alternate realities, alternate universes, all planetary systems, all Source systems, and all dimensions.

"I ask for the release of all crystals, devices, thought-forms, emotions, matrices, veils, cellular memory, pictures of reality, genetic limitation, and death — NOW!

"Under the Law of Grace and by the Decree of Victory! By the Decree of Victory! By the Decree of Victory!

"As Spirit wills, I ask for Awakening. As Spirit wills, we are awake!

"In the beginning, I AM THAT I AM! B'ray-sheet, Eh-yah esher Eh-yah!"

That clears out the attic and the basement. Now it's time to bring in new energy under your control. Time to contact Spirit!

8

Resonance 2:
Aligning with Spirit

The first question is, "Why am I not fully in contact with Spirit already, if my true nature is Spirit?"

Here's something else for which to take responsibility but not blame. At the moment you were born or walked in, you as Spirit did one of the most difficult and painful things in the universe: you incarnated on planet Earth. Nowhere on any other planet are the veils between the physical plane and the higher planes so dense. You knew, when you entered the body, that you would follow the rules that you helped set up for the species, and establish a point of focus which excluded the knowledge of who you were. You may have thought "No problem. I'll soon remember. And it's only for a few decades, anyway." So you slipped into a body, were squeezed through a tiny tunnel into a bright, cold world, were held upside down and smacked to make you breathe. Ouch! You drew the veils to forget that you were Spirit, and you've been trying to remember who you are ever since.

The first step in this recall involves accepting responsibility for forgetting in the first place. You could try this line of thinking for yourself:

> "I am Spirit. When I incarnated in this body, I voluntarily and purposefully forgot this in order to give myself this opportunity to rediscover it. I am Spirit, playing hide-and-seek with myself. My agreement was that once I knew this, the game would be over. I now know it and declare the game finished. I incarnated under these rules so that I could enjoy discovering my true nature. I am Spirit."

After a few repetitions and time to align all your fields to this truth, you will find your perception changing. You will begin to examine situations with, "I did this to learn more about being a limited human," "I invited this person into my life to share an experience," and "How does this insight serve me on my path to Light?"

With this, you have claimed your mastery! Instead of being Mary Jones, daughter, mate, mother, worker, and so on, you are Spirit performing the Mary Jones function, whatever that is. And the Mary Jones function should become apparent very quickly.

Acknowledge that you are here because, as Spirit, you wanted to be here. You had specific ideas about what you wanted to accomplish and it's time to review whether you're on track. It's time to become fully aware of, and align with, your spirit-self!

There are as many ways to embody Spirit as there are bodies. Each will be unique. However, there are some broad guidelines (but remember that it will not feel like "fireworks," because you never really disembodied Spirit, no matter how isolated you feel). You just forgot where to look. And if you've gotten this far, you've cleared away the energy patterns responsible for any resistance that could cause a "fireworks" type reaction.

We are grateful to Merlin for the following approach to embodying Spirit:

Unify your chakras and ask the appropriate level of Spirit to blend with your unified field through the heart chakra. Visualize a pink or red crystal in the heart chakra, glowing brightly. See it grow to just taller than you are. Approach it and touch it. You find that you can pass easily through its walls. It's just like pink light. Enter and look around. Someone is waiting to greet you. It's a figure that your spirit-self has projected. You will probably feel waves of love, compassion, and caring.

What you do next depends on you. You can just bask in this glow, ask questions, request guidance, or just make friends. Ask that this energy stay with you in your heart chakra and guide you in all that you do. Ask that you, as Spirit, blend with the unified field to keep it aligned and to embody an ever greater proportion of ever higher frequency energy. Finally, when you feel complete, let the image fade and return your consciousness to your surroundings. Affirm that "I am Spirit. I am a Master in all that I do."

Repeat this encounter as often as you wish. Feel free to set up your own encounters. Some people have a favorite place that they once visited and remember as special. Others build an inner place to go to. Something you imagine is no less real than a physical place or thing. The only difference is that the consensus reality doesn't include your private place, and since when have you felt constrained by the consensus?

Simply decree that when you arrive at your meeting place, your spirit-self will be there to greet your ego-self. You may encounter a figure that your ego finds appropriate — say, a very beautiful woman or a wise, compassionate man — but you should not be afraid of whatever appears. For example, you all have the energy of the archetypal aspects such as the Crone and the Reaper in you, and these aspects of your spirit function may have a valuable message for you. Keep firmly in mind that whomever or whatever you meet *is you* and welcome the opportunity to blend with that apparent other to the point where there is no distinction left.

A more specific technique, again from Ariel, can be used to follow Spirit and obtain insight about everyday issues in your physical plane life. It works on the basis that your mental body tends to live in the future, your emotional body in the past, and your physical body in the present.

Pose a question such as "How do I feel about taking job X?" or "How would marrying Y work out?"

Unify your chakras and invite Spirit to radiate from your heart into the unified chakra. Then imagine a door with the question written on it. Tell yourself that behind the door you are actually living the situation — the full, living, breathing, experiential situation. Behind the door, you've *already* taken job X or married person Y and it's irrevocable, with no turning back. It's now and it's real! How do you feel within your body? Relaxed, serene, happy, pleased at having made the right decision, or tense, anxious and upset that you've "screwed up" again? Your spirit-self has blended with your lower fields and, through resonance with the self that made that decision, has matched the energy to give you a taste of that particular out-come. That's why the body reacts as it does.

Before you leave, notice the door that has "Spirit's suggestion" written on it. The door may glow or sparkle and it feels like there's some good energy behind it. You may care to open it and go through. If you were asking earlier about a mate, you may meet him or her — possibly someone you've already met or a complete stranger! If you were asking about a job or a house, say, you may see yourself in a familiar setting or somewhere else. This may surprise you, but let it sit with you a while. How does your body feel now?

Remember that your personality always has choice. That was part of the deal. As Spirit, you hope for full and total merger but it must be bilaterally agreed upon and not a hostile takeover! But since you are now on the "fast track" to ascension, do you really want to take time out to explore choices that are not those of Spirit?

Simultaneous Time

This next technique gives you a sense of the structure of time from Spirit's perspective. In what follows, I capitalize NOW to emphasize that the NOW-point is the moment in time in which the you reading this book exists, rather than all the now-points which are not ordinarily accessible to your ego-self. Of course, all now-points are accessible to Spirit.

This NOW-point is where you are and where your power to deal with all planes lies. The previous now-point is gone and your ego-self can't go back and change anything. And the next now-point hasn't happened yet, so your ego-self can't do anything about that yet. You could imagine time as a narrow bridge across a chasm. Everything spreads out on either side, but focuses to a narrow point in the NOW. Your consciousness is the bridge between the past and the future. Everything must funnel through this narrow channel called NOW. The future flows through NOW to become the past. As it passes, you can change it, redefine it, amplify it, or deny it passage into the past as your personal history.

Imagine a situation that you want to change. See it coming toward you as you stand on the center of the bridge, requesting permission to cross over into your present. Tell it that it can only pass if it changes. Reconstruct it — be it a person, conversation, event, etc. — and then let it pass. You are actually changing the energy of that situation in the NOW-point.

This technique actually changes the blueprint for reality, making you a reality architect! Spirit operates all along the timeline in every now-point. Time is just another dimension and you can move in time as easily as you move in space. But just as the particular space which you occupy acts as a focal point, the NOW-point in which your ego-self exists is also a focal point to your spirit-self. This NOW-point is the meeting ground for ego and spirit-selves. It is the point of unity where you can exercise your full personal power.

Wishing that something will come true in the future is futile. Your ego is trying to jump the timeline and has no power to act in the future. It's like trying to lift something heavy when you're off balance. You've no leverage and may fall over.

So how do you influence a "future" now-point from this NOW-point? Through your field! If you unify your chakras and the three lower fields and invite Spirit into the unified field, you can get to that other now-point.

Suppose, for example, that you are interviewing for a new job tomorrow, a job you really want. Unify your chakras and invite Spirit to radiate from your heart into the unified chakra. Then imagine a door, as you did before. Behind the door, you've already taken job X.

Check behind the door to make sure that this one really feels good at all levels and is in alignment with Spirit (this alignment is important because if you and your new boss do not have a spirit-to-spirit agreement to work together, tomorrow will just be interviewing practice. If you *do* have such an agreement, you'll have to work hard *not* to get the job!). It's no use scripting the interview ahead of time — that just locks you into a mental body pattern. Instead, sit down quietly and pull your field into this NOW-point and space. Become a tight focus of physical, emotional, mental, and spirit energy. Now, if you know what the job entails and what you would be doing, then see, think, and feel yourself doing it NOW, not in the future. Make it as realistic as possible. Conjure up the smells and sounds of the office or work site. Bring it all to this NOW-point. After a few minutes, bring your consciousness back.

What happened? You created a resonance between two now-points in simultaneity. You tapped into the energy of a future now-point from your current NOW-point. By doing so, you increase the intensity of your NOW-point energy fields by pulling some of the energy of the probability of getting the job into your NOW-point. You and the interviewer have, at some future now-point, got to make a hiring decision. Many probability lines emanate from that decision-point and you selected the energy associated with one of them and folded it back into the present.

Several things come out of this. By involving your spirit-self in the exercise, you also involved the interviewer's spirit-self and those of the people with whom you would be working. Actual interviews are always preceded by "psychic" interviews, often while you sleep. By previewing the job situation, you've become a conscious player and added your intent to the probability pie.

You may have had an adverse reaction during the exercise, such as coughing, tight breathing, or muscle tension. This indicates that you may wish to review your intent. Some energy in that "future" field disagreed with you. It may be the energy of a potential co-worker or toxins in the building's air. Just stay open and ask yourself what the symptoms indicate.

Now, say there are three possible outcomes to the interview: you get the job on your terms, on their terms, or not at all (and remember that the latter may be the most appropriate outcome — your twin flame may be working for the next employer or client you interview with!). See these three lines diverging from a point, or visualize three doors marked with the options. Tell yourself that you want the line or door that brings the most joy. One may light up more than the others. If so, go inside the line or door and feel what it's like. If none lights up, reconsider attending the interview — it's certainly not on Spirit's calendar.

That ego of yours in the future now-point is as real as you are right now. He or she exists in flesh and bone, but is just not accessible from your current vantage point. So, change your vantage point. Move your point of focus to that of Spirit and take a look at what you're up to in that now-point. With practice, you will soon be able to maintain two points of focus in the NOW-point, of two different now-points.

Extend this to three, then four now-points. Soon you will get the feeling of being spread across time like a layer of oil on water. You'll find that your "presence" thickens at certain points — these are your co-incarnees. Send them love and encouragement. Imagine what your presence feels like to them!

You have entered the realm of simultaneous time — a true Spirit perspective — and can influence any event, whether "past" or "future," through resonance. Suppose you encounter a self in Atlantis wavering between identifying with Spirit or ego. Just the contact with your unified field will, through resonance, help prevent the "soul/spirit split" from happening in that lifetime. That self may be in the priesthood and go on to influence countless contemporaries.

So, in simultaneous time, we dispel the idea that what's happened has happened and can't be changed, and that the future hasn't happened yet, so can't be changed yet. You can change it, even if you don't know what you're doing, by remaining firmly anchored in the present and using resonance to work on either side of the NOW-point. Your unified field works in ways you don't consciously know.

In summary, then, there are many techniques that the blend of ego and Spirit can use to align and merge. Play at inventing new ones and share them with others.

In the next chapter, we begin to explore unity further — unity with everything because, you see, you were never *other* than everything. One thing you will hear more and more frequently is that Spirit is a unity, a continuum of energy — admittedly organized in indescribable ways, but a unity nevertheless. It is only "function" that looks separate.

═══ **9**

Unity

The physical plane is an odd place to be. Everything seems so separate. Each person walks around thinking that they begin and end at the surface of their skin. Objects look as though they have distinct edges and surfaces. Events seem to have a distinct beginning and end. None of this is true!

Your personal fields extend anywhere from several feet to several miles around you, depending on your intent and which frequency band we are referring to. You extend in frequency from the dense standing waves of your physical body (which the physical senses fool you into thinking is solid) up to the highest frequencies of pure love, which set up this and every universe.

The objects in your life are made of pure energy, excitedly buzzing about and emitting or reflecting heat and light. You see this, and with equally energetic hands, you feel objects. In one of the most brilliantly creative processes in the universe, your brain pieces together this data about energy and registers it as something solid.

The events in your life are complex webs of association. An apparently chance meeting of an old acquaintance on a downtown street corner may have been agreed upon before you were both born. As Spirit, you may have planned to each acquire certain skills and knowledge, and then to meet again so that one of you could offer a job to the other, or to grow in compatibility and begin a relationship, which could end in becoming mated.

So, looked at from Spirit's perspective (and you will be doing so more and more by now), there are no individuals, no separate things, and no isolated events. There is only energy flowing back and forth, and up and down in frequency.

The next question, then, may be "If this is true, how do I get into the flow and become conscious of this Everything?"

Unity Band

We've talked a lot about the various fields and frequency bands. Remember that the dimensions are not places, but frequency bands like those used for police, aircraft, or commercial radio, etc. They support a different type of energy, of a much higher frequency, but the idea is the same.

Ariel offers the following twelve-dimensional model to guide us through the dimensions:

Your physical body exists in the third dimension — it's matter-based. The fourth dimension is the astral plane — it's emotion-based. Together these two make up what we call the Lower Creation World. These are the dimensions where the game of separation is carried out. Only in these dimensions can the illusion of good and evil be maintained and can you feel separated from Spirit and from each other. You've all become quite good at doing that. It's been a very successful game of separation but now it's time for it to end. So, this planet is in a state of ascension. It's now vibrating at the very top of the astral plane, right on the dividing line with the fifth dimension — the Lightbody dimension. As part of the ascension process, these dimensions will be rolled up into the higher dimensions and will cease to exist.

The fifth through the ninth dimensions make up the Mid-Creation Realm. The fifth is the Lightbody dimension in which you are aware of yourself as a Master and a multi-dimensional being. In the fifth dimension, you are completely spiritually oriented. Many of you have come in from this plane to be Lightworkers.

The sixth dimension holds the templates for the DNA patterns of all types of species' creation, including humankind. It's also where the Light languages are stored and is made up mostly of color and tone. It is the dimension where consciousness creates through thought and one of the places where you work during sleep. It can be difficult to get a bead on this because you're not in a body unless you choose to create one. When you are operating sixth-dimensionally, you are more of an alive thought. You create through your consciousness, but you don't necessarily have a vehicle for that consciousness.

The seventh dimension is that of pure creativity, pure light, pure tone, pure geometry, and pure expression. It is a plane of infinite refinement.

The eighth is the dimension of group mind or group soul and where you would touch base with the vaster part of who you are. It is characterized by loss of sense of the "I." When you travel multi-dimensionally, it's this plane where you have most trouble keeping your consciousness together because you are pure "we," operating with group goals. So, it may seem as though you've gone to sleep or blanked out.

The ninth dimension in the model that we use is the plane of the collective consciousness of planets, star systems, galaxies and dimensions. Once again, it's very difficult to get a sense of "I" because you are so vast that everything is "you." Imagine being the consciousness of a galaxy. Every life-form, every star, planet, and group mind of every species in it is you. If you visit this dimension, it can be difficult to remain conscious.

The tenth through twelfth dimensions make up the Upper Creation Realm. The tenth is the source of the Rays, home of what are called the Elohim. This is where Light is differentiated and is the source of plans of creation which are sent to the Mid-Creation levels. You can have a sense of "I" at this level but it won't be what you're used to here. The eleventh dimension is that of preformed Light — the point before creation and a state of exquisite expectancy just like the moment before a sneeze or an orgasm. It is the realm of the being known as Metatron, and of Archangels and the Higher Akashic for this Source-system. There are planetary Akashic records and galactic Akashics as well as the Akashic for *an entire Source-system. You are in one Source-system of many. So, we are giving you a description of one Source-system only — this one. If you go to another Source-system, what you will experience will be different. As an Archangel, my home base is the eleventh dimension. We come to you as messengers — that's what "Archangel" means. It's one of my functions — I have many. I have an Elohim function which is not very verbal. We have many, many jobs.*

The twelfth-dimension is the One Point where all consciousness knows itself to be utterly one with All That Is. There is no separation of any kind. If you tap into this level, you know yourself to be completely one with All That Is, with the creator force. If you tap in there, you will never be the same again because you cannot sustain the same degree of separation if you have experienced complete unity.

Spirit creates the illusion of separation up to the seventh dimension; at higher frequencies, distinctions become completely meaningless and all is Spirit. A definite frequency band exists in all these levels which acts as a unifying medium, a common frequency — like the public channel on CB radio, except that you don't just talk on it but you are part of it. If you match your consciousness to the frequency of this Unity Band, you experience complete unity with all that is. It is also known as the Christed Band and emanates from the Christed level. It throws off subharmonics into all the lower frequency planes. The energy in the Christed level is your energy. It is the level at which you exist as a Christed Being, above separateness. For the sake of convenience, we often term this unity function the Office of the Christ, and in Earth's history, this function has manifested directly in human form without intermediate levels of Spirit. You know these beings as Quetzalcoatl, Hiawatha, Lao-Tzu, Krishna, Buddha, and Jesus. They are direct projections of the Unity Band and appeared at different points in history to change the course of events by reminding mankind of its unity. We also use the name Sananda as the Christ Collective.

The Unity Band therefore is a frequency and its subharmonics occur in all planes or dimensions. If you attune to that frequency, you just know unity — it isn't even an issue. Attuning to the subharmonics is like taking an elevator to the top floor: quick, direct, and effective. The doors open and the wave of love swamps you.

Sananda has given us ways of finding our way to the elevator and I have invited Sananda to address you directly:

I am Sananda. I come to you from the level at which you are One. My purpose is to help you experience the level of joy of your higher frequency aspects. First, it is appropriate to correct a few misinterpretations which arose from the language and beliefs of earlier times.

I have been quoted as saying that "None shall reach the Father but through me." What was really meant by that was that to experience your true nature, or I AM self, you must first align with the Unity Band frequency that I create from my energy.

I have also been quoted as saying, "Suffer the little children to come unto me." Again this was mistranslated. What was meant was that in order to experience unity, be as free of fear, mental images, judgements, living in the past or future, as children are. These things block your entry to the unity experience.

Several things happened on your planet in 1988 which make direct experience of unity now possible. First, I established the elevator that Serapis mentioned, right down to the lower planes, so that you can sense subharmonic frequencies of my energy within your own field. Reciting the following invocation will tune you to that frequency and you can then direct your perception to match the harmonics of that frequency on each of the higher levels. When you have reached the Unity Band, you will know: a sense of peace and oneness will wash over you.

Second, the energy of Grace has been brought onto this planet. This is the energy of the Silver Ray, the ray of harmony and blending. Whatever you are doing to increase the frequency of energy in your personal fields will go more smoothly if you invoke Grace. Simply imagine a beam of silver light, bright and sparkling, flowing into your fields, washing away whatever low frequency energy you don't want. It will calm you if you are agitated or enliven you if you are tired.

A third major change was the removal of continuity. Throughout the history of Earth, the Orange Ray has fueled the mass thoughtforms of the consensus reality necessary to support the karma game and the status quo. The Orange Ray was purified in late 1988 and immediately, old patterns of hostility on Earth began to crumble, no longer held in place. You are now free to change as fast as you wish.

I thank Serapis for this opportunity to greet you. In love and unity, I am Sananda.

Invocation to Unity

We offer the following invocation to help you tap into the Unity Band:

> I am a Christed Being; I am in unity with Spirit
> I am a Christed Being; I am in unity with All That Is;
> The Light of my own Being shines upon my path
> I am a Christed Being; I am in unity with All That Will Be
> I hold the shining Light of the Source within my heart
> I walk in unity with Spirit
> I laugh in unity with the Source
> I love in unity with my fellow beings
> I am a Christed Spirit; I am a bridge between heaven and Earth

The function you know as Sananda has created a "consciousness elevator" through the planes — a set of harmonic frequencies. Using this set of frequencies, you can experience Unity. Sananda usually projects as a very kind and gentle being, to allow your emotional body to relate to the function and the underlying unity. When Spirit performs this function, it undertakes to communicate as a particular loving being, although the Sananda function is no more or less loving than any other.

When Spirit enacted the historical Christ, Buddha, and Krishna functions, for example, it expressed the unity and unconditional love of the Source through these forms — human beings just like you who had cleared the lower fields and unified them sufficiently to handle the high frequency energy of the upper dimensions. This comes automatically when two things happen: first, you love yourself unconditionally, and second, you know that you are in unity with all that is. Then, unconditional love is inevitable. Being one with Spirit, you are made of exactly the same "stuff" as those historical figures, and your spirit-stuff does indeed perform the Sananda or Christ function.

The historical figure of Jesus was an incarnation of an Ascended Master whose fields were sufficiently clear to allow the high-frequency energy of Spirit (from the Christed dimension) to blend with his fields, to the extent that he was able to perform the Christ/Sananda function on the physical plane. In that lifetime, he was such an open channel that Spirit was able to embody the Christ energy in his fields. Anyone coming within his field was flooded with that energy and, if they in turn were open enough, could experience that energy through resonance.

Those whose fields contained any energy that was not of self-love — such as guilt, self-recrimination, or self-blame — felt very uncomfortable in his presence, even though Unity Band energy is, itself, totally non-judgemental. On the one hand, Christ energy amplifies love of self and others, and raises its frequency even higher. On the other hand, energy not of love of self and others is revealed in stark relief and you are forced to acknowledge it. If you are unwilling to accept it as yours, you may project the anger, hatred, bitterness, and fear out onto a convenient target. Jesus was such a target, of course. It is ironic but true that when faced with Unity, people project their feelings of disunity onto the source of the unity. Thus the biblical figure of Jesus was seen as divisive.

Be aware, therefore, that when you experience the Unity Band energy for the first time, you may feel the exact opposite of unity. Don't worry. Be glad that you can feel the energy of separateness in your fields: old imprinting laid down over the years that you can now dump.

Here's a technique you can try:

Unify your chakras and fields, and blend with your spirit-function. Imagine your consciousness going up an elevator from the physical plane. See the floor names blink as you ascend the planes. Stop at the Christ Level. As the doors open, allow your consciousness to move out of the elevator. You will probably see several people — some you know, and some you don't. They are projections of high-frequency aspects of their spirit-selves and they already experience full unity with you. How do you feel about them? Can you sense the unity or do you feel separate?

If you encounter someone from whom you feel separate, try a dialog along these lines:

"I acknowledge that I feel separation. I am a Master and built this in as a learning tool. It is no longer useful, and I release it back to the universe. I choose instead to experience Unity. I now know and feel my unity with all that is. You, [whatever their name is], and I are Spirit, united and indivisible."

Roam around freely, greeting whomever you meet. Feel free to invite Sananda to appear. You created the space and can invite in anyone you like. When you feel complete, return to the elevator and bring your consciousness back to your unified field.

This dialog is also very useful any time you are at odds with someone. In the middle of a heated debate at work or during a row with your mate or child, try to project these words to his or her spirit-self from your heart chakra. You already know that he or she is within your unified field and *will* get the message at some level.

Remember, you can go back any time you wish. You will return a little different each time — I guarantee it!

Being All That You Are

We've covered enough ground by now for you to have a good idea of who you really are. The next question that arises may be, "How do I express this larger self?" or "How can I *be* this larger self?"

The Greek root of the word "enthusiasm" is "en" and "theos" which literally means "in God." Anything about which you feel enthused is in Spirit and automatically brings you joy. Anything that does not bring you joy is not in Spirit. Ask yourself why you're doing it, whether it's a job you hate or feeling sick. You are in Spirit if you're feeling joy. The trick is to become fully aware of how you *feel* about things as distinct from what you think about them or think you should feel. Physical, emotional, and mental clarity are essential in order to allow you to fully manifest Spirit.

You'll find that your intuitive senses become very acute. You'll just know things that you haven't heard or read about, and couldn't deduce, like what's coming in the mail, or who's on the other end of the ringing telephone. Trust this and play with it.

You'll find yourself dreaming lucidly, that is, knowing that you are dreaming during the dream. Then you can really begin to play, because dreams are the arena in which you, as Spirit, create and manipulate reality on all planes. You also preview the events in your physical plane life and decide which experiences to manifest physically. You and everyone else on this planet first create your waking reality in your dreams. What fun to consciously manipulate this emergent reality before it happens physically!

Your ability to manifest things and people into your life will increase to the point where, ultimately, you think or feel something and it happens. Now you see why mental and emotional clarity is so important.

In countless little things during the day, you'll see the hand of Spirit at work, or more aptly, at play (you've been doing this all the time, of course, but you didn't stand far enough back to see the patterns that you created from the level of your spirit-self). Being free of the fear that blocks flow, Spirit can work through you without resistance or distortion. And I mean Spirit rather than spirit-self. I'm talking about the entire realm of Spirit, from archangel to the spirit in your cat, dog, and houseplant.

If anything happens in your life which you would prefer didn't, you catch it quickly and ask "How does this serve ascension?" Once you find out, the situation generally changes very quickly.

You'll feel part of the universe rather than separate. As you pass a tree, for example, you'll sense the devic energy and enjoy a little exchange between the two of you. You'll begin to sense the magic of being alive, of being in the flow. Soon the sense of peace and elation you found only in meditation will pervade your entire life. Every encounter with your fellow men will be a loving, healing occasion. And you will be able to freely contact any nonphysical entity you wish, to exchange information or just schmooze. Your sense of appropriateness will guide you in your daily life, and you'll know just what to do. And after you've finished this book, you'll give it to someone else because there's nothing else it can tell you that you do not know from Spirit.

But before that, let's look at your higher-frequency self again in a little more detail.

We saw earlier that our Mary Jones is really Spirit performing the Mary Jones function. Now this function exists up through all the bands, each one a higher aspect of Mary Jones. If Mary wants to be all that she is, how does she discover what this is?

Simple. She asks herself at that frequency. Here's how:

Unify your chakras and ask the appropriate-level of your Spirit to blend with the lower fields (it/you knows what's coming so it /you knows what to do). Meet in the pink crystal, and ask yourself to show your conscious mind what goes on at these higher frequencies. You will see pictures, hear voices, and get an intuitive sense of what a certain level of Spirit does when it is performing the type of function we've been talking about.

There's no way to predict what you'll see and experience. You may see yourself moving about in a large grid of bright filaments, weaving new connections as you evaluate and select probabilities. You may be in a planning meeting to decide on the basis for a new planet, or teaching higher mathematics in a large building made of crystals that glow from within. Trust that you're not making it up. Spirit really does do these things — you included — whether you're consciously aware of it or not. (So much for your spirit being something you "have." You have a full life at these levels, and it is more true to say that your spirit-self is something that has you!)

Now, initially you may not know what's going on. You may see yourself and wonder, "How did I know to put that probability line there, and what is it the probability *of*, anyway?" Don't worry. As you spend more time in the higher planes, your ability to consciously match frequency with who you're watching will increase and you'll just know by direct cognition. It may take a few months, but you'll get there because it's really you doing this stuff.

This high frequency aspect of you may take you traveling through the planes, to other planets, or even to other universes where the rules are all different. By now, it's up to you. You are a Master, in control of everything you experience. These adventures all end the same way, however. You finish up back in your physical field. It's only been your consciousness that's been to the higher planes. But not for long. That brings us to ascension!

═══11

Ascension

Now that you've aligned the physical, emotional, mental, and spirit fields, achieved full internal resonance among them to the point of having unified them, and have achieved a high degree of resonance with the higher frequencies of Spirit, it's time to begin ascension in earnest (you have been engaged in ascension all along: it is a process, not an event).

As we saw earlier, ascension is the process of raising the frequency of all the energy in your lower fields, including the cells of your physical body, so that they contain no energy which vibrates on the lower planes at all. Your lowest energy frequency — currently the physical body — is then in the fifth dimension. Others in this band can see your energy clearly and hear you telepathically but not audibly, because you cannot make sounds (air is too dense for fifth-dimensional vocal cords to move). You are, of course, not visible from the physical plane. Your energy is just too high a frequency to register on the physical retina. So you have "disappeared," but you can still affect the physical plane.

First, you can readily project your Light Body anywhere on the physical plane. Second, while you've been busy ascending, your friends have been practicing their channeling and now you're "it." Your wisdom after achieving alignment makes you a popular entity to channel. Having only recently been physical and having gone through the process yourself, you are ideally equipped to assist them in clearing the blocks on their path, just as you were helped by other entities on your path. And the very fact that you achieved this frequency shift will encourage others. The process of planetary ascension will accelerate geometrically as each new Ascended Master helps a few hundred ascendees.

When you're not facilitating others, you'll still have your own show going on. Ascending to the fifth dimension is a major step, but by no means the last. But you'll have stopped reading books long before then, so it's not appropriate for me to talk about what you can expect as you continue your ascension.

How then, do you raise your base frequencies to those of the fifth dimension? Ascension involves raising the frequency of the energy making up your fields. This energy is the energy behind the electromagnetic spectrum of which light is a part — it is the energy that bursts through the physical barrier to become electromagnetic radiation and ultimately to appear as subatomic particles or waves — it is the Light behind light.

The consciousness making up your subatomics already knows this, and never stepped away from conscious union with the Source for an instant. But it agreed to conform with the lower-frequency envelopes making up your personality. So the trick is to raise the frequency of your cellular consciousness to match. Then your body will no longer think that it's going to die (death has been the end of every lifetime so far, so you can't blame the poor body for thinking this).

You transmute your energy by intent. It's that simple. If your four fields are aligned and they hold the intent that something is true, the lowest frequency field, the physical, has to change or it will be out of alignment. So through your intent, you raise the frequencies of the energy in the physical field by an octave, and another, and another. You can do this. Remember how you lowered your frequency a few octaves to densify into the physical a long time ago. Now, admittedly, that took a long time because your physical body is an enormously complex chemical plant, controlled by DNA, communicating with hormones, and dealing with high-tech organic compounds within critical limits. (Have you ever stopped to ponder how your body maintains its temperature at exactly 98.6 degrees? Imagine what went into planning that!) Of course it took eons to figure it all out, and there were many false starts and dead ends. But with ascension, you know and your body consciousness knows where you're going — your fifth-dimensional Lightbody is the blueprint, and it already exists! You could do this at this very moment if you wished.

Once your fields are aligned, you'll be able to set your intent to increase the vibratory rate of your cellular structures at will. You will boost your intent by clear visualization of light flooding into the cells and DNA, and by imprinting your cells with images of cells made up of extremely high-frequency energy. Your body will literally become light, as the cells absorb this high-frequency energy and start to emit light themselves.

Now, in simultaneous time, the you who will ascend is already there, enjoying every moment of it. You can accelerate your conscious arrival at those frequencies through field resonance. The "fifth-dimensional you" wants you to accelerate because that means that he or she (or it — you can appear however you want, remember) needed less time to get there and began to enjoy the party earlier (this is said for the benefit of the conscious mind, not the fifth-dimensional self).

The lowest frequency that your fifth-dimensional self expresses through is obviously now in the fifth dimension, and you can easily reach this by clarity and intent. Your fields will then resonate at the fifth-dimensional frequencies and foster the skills, knowledge, wisdom, and love in your fields. Your physical, emotional, and mental fields will vibrate in harmony with your fifth-dimensional self, which is already partying away. This will get you to the party much sooner.

Unify your chakras and invite the fifth-dimensional level of your spirit-self to blend with your field. Set your intent to show your conscious mind what life on the fifth dimension is like, through visions, words, sensations, or just knowing. Then try to hold the double consciousness of being here and there simultaneously. Experiment with changing your focus between the two realities. Enter fully into the fifth-dimensional reality. Be there. Your unified field will resonate with the fifth-dimensional energy and your physical field energy will lighten in resonance with the higher harmonics of your fifth-dimensional body. Your emotional field will resonate with the love in your fifth-dimensional field, and your mental field will flood with the wisdom of your fifth-dimensional self. You will come out of the experience a very different person, closer to the being you are, and are becoming.

This may seem a little far out to you, but that doesn't matter. When you get to this stage in your ascension process, it will seem quite normal. I do not intend describing the ascension process itself. I could write an entire book about making ice cream and the last line would simply be "Eat it." You'll know how when you get there. And I shall be waiting for you.

Life After Ascension

O bviously, if you're still reading, you're interested in the process and may want to know where it's leading (or maybe you got curious and turned straight to this chapter). So, I am closing this book by giving you a glimpse of what you can expect after ascension. Remember that a part of you is already on the fifth dimension — the rest of you is about to catch up.

Life on the fifth dimension is very different from what you experience now. Space, time, obstructions, and limitations play a large part of your life today. Imagine if they weren't there. What would it be like?

In Lightbody, you know who you really are: a pure loving being, united with all other beings as part of the Source, but still sufficiently individuated to be able to say to another being "We are both the Source" (at higher frequencies, concepts like "we" and "both" are meaningless).

You know who you are in terms of your incarnations across time, what you're learning from each, and how each is a bold and daring mission through which the Source learns more about itself. As Spirit, you automatically broadcast whatever you learn through all frequency bands, so that your discoveries can be enjoyed through direct cognition. That's why each tiny detail of your life is so important: you are a discoverer and explorer for the entire universe.

You are a master of creation. Your thoughts are instantly implemented as objects, music, art, and other exquisite forms to be enjoyed by other fifth-dimensional beings. However, the textures, colors, sounds, and materials you have at your disposal are literally unlimited. If you're musically inclined, you could create an organ with a range and depth of tone beyond anything on the physical plane, because it doesn't work by moving air about but by amplifying your thoughts and emotions.

If you're artistically inclined, the colors available to you are not limited to pigments which reflect and absorb visible light. You can paint with light itself, impressing your vision directly onto multi-dimensional space that you create.

A mathematician can project an algebraic equation into a space created with as many dimensions as necessary. Geometry comes alive as you express complex shapes as sounds or colors.

You create your own place to "live" as a meeting point for your fifth-dimensional friends, a place that is every bit as real as your physical plane home. The only difference is that you can redecorate it with a thought and change the view by your intent.

You can have a lot of fun trying on different body types. At this frequency, your body is pure thought projection but, again, every bit as real to you as your physical body is now. You can project the body of one of your favorite incarnations of either sex and make love with infinitely more sensation than with physical bodies. And you can surprise your friends by projecting an off-planet body. Amuse them by waving your eighteen tentacles at them, shock them with a real Kizn growl, and impress them by becoming Mount Olympus.

What you can do is limited only by what you want to do, and what brings you joy. The most significant difference is that, being free of any fear-based frequencies, you express the pure unconditional love of the Source. There is no barrier between you and the Source, and I can't even hint at the ecstasy that comes with that. You can ask Spirit to give you a taste of it during meditation, but that's a bit like smelling the food outside a good restaurant.

You may be wondering if ascension means leaving the physical plane altogether. The answer is "No." Admittedly the lowest frequency of your being is in the fifth dimension and therefore invisible to those remaining on the physical plane. However, you can project a visible Light Body at will. It is a little more ethereal than a physical body, and it will glow a little, which may surprise others and never fail to get you a seat on public transit. You may choose to project the body you hold now, to make others feel comfortable, but if you've always wanted to be "Marie Antoinette" ... ! Your full fifth-dimensional consciousness is associated with this Light Body and you may care to show up for speaking engagements, just hang out with your old friends, or drop in on Congress for the day. You will have the wisdom of appropriateness in all that you do — you are an Ascended Master after all!

Postscript

I have said that there is no such thing as a stand-alone event in your life. What seem to be events are just tiny pieces of much larger processes, intruding into the physical plane. Ascension, too, is not an event, but a huge process that began with the original densification. Planetary ascension was inevitable from the moment you, on the various Creation Councils, conceived of the glorious experiment you call planet Earth. Only the timing was debatable. Even then, Spirit, in the Infinite Now, was planning for these few final years and juggling probabilities. Well, the results are almost in. All probability lines point to planetary ascension within a few years, and by the end of the millennium at the latest.

You can help yourself and the planet by accelerating your personal ascension and not waiting until the last moment. Take this to heart (literally), and begin your personal ascension now. We are with you.

— I am Serapis.

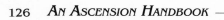

Appendix:
An Ascension Toolkit

This appendix describes some invaluable Lightworker tools brought on to the planet by Archangel Ariel through Tachiren of Angelic Outreach (reproduced by permission). They have proved useful for both individual and group work.

1. *The Principle of Asking*

By Universal Law, no higher-dimensional being can intercede or assist you unless you request it. Develop the habit of asking for assistance, information, and guidance.

2. *Grace It and Get On With It!*

Grace is a divine force that allows a complete break with the past and a fresh start in each now-moment. Grace Elohim holds the energies of divine joy, forgiveness, gratitude, and celebration. She looks like iridescent snow and immediately intercedes if you ask her to. Because of the Universal Law that the universe rearranges itself according to your pictures of reality, we encourage people not to "process," but instead to "Grace it and get on with it."

3. *Invocation to Light*

I live within the Light.
I love within the Light.
I laugh within the Light.
I AM sustained and nourished by the Light.
I joyously serve the Light.
For I AM the Light.
I AM the Light. I AM the Light. I AM. I AM. I AM.

4. *Invocation to Water*

I take this the Water of Life.
I declare it the Water of Light.
As I bring it within my body,
It allows my body to glow.
I take this the Water of Light.
I declare it the Water of God.
I AM a Master in all that I AM.

5. *The Violet Flame*

St. Germain, Lord of the Violet Ray, offers the violet flame of transmutation for dealing with low-frequency energy you wish to remove from your fields. Use it whenever you are dropping density of any kind or when you encounter low-frequency energy in your environment. Do it several times a day if necessary.

For personal use, visualize the violet flame of transmutation (mixed with the Silver Ray of Grace to form a beautiful iridescent violet). Then see it pouring into your physical body and filling every cell. Then bring it through your emotional, mental and spiritual bodies separately.

To clean a space, such as your office or home, see the violet flames rising up from the floor, consuming all low-frequency energy. Pay particular attention to cleaning your bed when you get up in the morning.

6. *Spiritual Hygiene*

Use sea salt and the Violet Flame, mixed with Grace, to clean your fields. Place sea salt and invoke the rays into your bath water. Wash your clothes and bed-linens with a handful of sea salt to remove energetic residue. Because you do most of your clearing in your sleep, call in the above rays to transmute the old energies as you make your bed. You'll feel so much better.

7. *Grounding Up*

If your level of Lightbody is way ahead of that of the planet, the traditional way of grounding into the planet will feel very uncomfortable. Instead, try grounding up into your spirit-self. Imagine a thick line of Light beginning at your Omega chakra, extending upwards through your spine and on upwards to the eleventh chakra. Grounding into the vastness of your Spirit allows your Spirit to stabilize you.

8. *Toning*

Toning is a technology and language for the multidimensional transmission of Light, color, motion, and geometries. Toning breaks up dysfunctional patterns, transmutes lifetimes of karma, infuses new patterns, and feels GOOD!

9. *Invocation to the Unified Chakra*

Use this invocation to get centered, before using any of the other tools, and before performing any activity involving Spirit. Unifying to the tenth chakra is often sufficient, but on occasion, you may want to unify to the twelfth and invite the Christ Oversoul into your fields. Pay particular attention to opening your Alpha and Omega chakras.

I breathe in Light through the center of my heart,
Opening my heart into a beautiful ball of Light,
Allowing myself to expand.

I breathe in Light through the center of my heart,
Allowing the Light to expand,
Encompassing my throat chakra
And my solar plexus chakra
In one unified field of Light
Within, through, and around my body.

I breathe in Light through the center of my heart,
Allowing the Light to expand,
Encompassing my brow chakra
And my navel chakra
In one unified field of Light
Within, through, and around my body.

{ ... *more* ...}

I breathe in Light through the center of my heart,
Allowing the Light to expand,
Encompassing my crown chakra
And my base chakra
In one unified field of Light
Within, through, and around my body.

I breathe in Light through the center of my heart,
Allowing the Light to expand,
Encompassing my Alpha chakra above my head,
And my Omega chakra below my spine
In one unified field of Light
Within, through, and around my body.
I allow the Wave of Metatron to resonate between them.
I AM a unity of Light.

I breathe in Light through the center of my heart,
Allowing the Light to expand,
Encompassing my eighth chakra above my head,
And my thighs
In one unified field of Light
Within, through, and around my body.
I allow my emotional body to merge with my physical.
I AM a unity of Light.

I breathe in Light through the center of my heart,
Allowing the Light to expand,
Encompassing my ninth chakra above my head,
And my calves
In one unified field of Light
Within, through, and around my body.
I allow my mental body to merge with my physical.
I AM a unity of Light.

I breathe in Light through the center of my heart,
Allowing the Light to expand,

{ ... *more* ...}

Encompassing my tenth chakra above my head,
And to below my feet
In one unified field of Light
Within, through, and around my body.
I allow my spiritual body to merge with my physical.
I AM a unity of Light.

I breathe in Light through the center of my heart,
Allowing the Light to expand,
Encompassing my eleventh chakra above my head,
And to below my feet
In one unified field of Light within, through, and
around my body.
I allow my Oversoul to merge with my physical.
I AM a unity of Light.

I breathe in Light through the center of my heart,
Allowing the Light to expand,
Encompassing my twelfth chakra above my head,
And to below my feet
In one unified field of Light
Within, through, and around my body.
I allow the Christ Oversoul to merge with my physical.
I AM a unity of Light.

I breathe in Light through the center of my heart,
I ask that the highest level of my Spirit radiate forth
From the center of my heart,
Filling this unified field completely.
I radiate forth throughout this day.
I AM unity of Spirit.

10. Protection

To protect your fields against unwanted intrusion by
detrimental energies, use the following three-step
process at least morning and evening, and whenever
you feel like extra protection, such as at work or on the
freeway:

- After you've unified your chakras and created the unified field, cover the outside of the field with gold mesh. State that the gold mesh will let only love and Light in and out.

- Call on the Legions of Michael, the Destroyer Angels, and Circle Security, in turn, to lay in a triple protective grid around you and your home or office.

- Ask the Destroyer Angels to spin out any detrimental energies from your fields.

11. *Synchronizing*

Your various energy bodies rotate at very particular rates, and the rates of spin are usually harmonics and subharmonics of each other, such as 11, 22, 33, and 44. When one of your fields begins to spin off its normal rate, you may feel dizzy.

Unify your chakras to the tenth, and try to sense the spin of each field in turn. One field may feel faster or slower, or just not right. Use your intent and vary the speed of this field, sensing the effect, until you feel that your fields are in synch again. If you have trouble with this, just ask Spirit to do it for you.

(There are many other causes of dizziness, of course, so see a physician if the symptom persists; this explanation is neither a medical diagnosis nor a recommendation for treatment.)

12. *Boogie Busting*

Feel any resistance, fear, anger, neediness, cravings, obsessions, or addictions, especially when you are trying to work with Spirit? Then you've probably got boogies. These are usually astral critters, either camping out with you because they are attracted by your Light, or because you invited them in a long time ago to keep you limited and human.

To remove them, first, call on your friends on the fifth dimension and above: Archangels Ariel, Azrael, and Arukiri, Polaria, Lord Michael, and anyone else you wish. Ask for, and visualize, Lord Michael sending a tube of Light from the fifth dimension to around your energy bodies. Then say:

"I release all agreements, both conscious and unconscious, with any detrimental entity, astral entity, or boogie. Please go into the Light. Now!"

Make it fun; put them on rollerskates or throw a bon voyage party. You are assisting a brother or sister to go home.

Thank the boogie for its work in keeping you limited, and tell it that the limitation is no longer appropriate. Then ask it to go up the Light tube. Be firm. If you feel resistance, demand that the boogie stand in front of you and tell you what it wants from you. It may be just recognition, or it may need reassurance that it has served its purpose well. Get increasingly firm that it must leave, shouting out loud if necessary. Feel your energy bodies. Do they feel lighter everywhere or is there still a heaviness or pain anywhere? If you still feel heavy, consult a professional boogie-buster.

When you feel lighter everywhere, begin to tone. This will release the last remaining energy and help them up to the fifth dimension. Then ask Lord Michael to collapse the tube away from your bodies into the fifth dimension.

13. Channeling

We encourage everyone to learn to channel. This allows you to get your own multi-dimensional information, keeps you in constant contact with a wider perspective, and breaks down reliance on outside authority. Besides, it's ecstatic and fun!

14. Superconscious

This technique was brought in by Earth Mission and is very effective in changing pictures of reality.

"Superconscious, by the force of Grace, will you manifest the essence of the effect and performance, and embodiment of the highest possibility of [the new picture of reality you wish to assimilate], so that the

power of this can be manifest in my experience. By the force of Grace and by the decree of Victory. And so it is!"

15. *The Great Invocation*

From the point of Light within the mind of God
Let light stream forth into the minds of men.
Let light descend on Earth.

From the point of Love within the heart of God
Let Love stream forth into the hearts of men.
May Christ return to Earth.

From the center where the Will of God is known
Let the purpose guide the little wills of men —
The purpose which the Masters know and serve.

From the center which we call the race of men
Let the Plan of Love and Light work out
And may it seal the door where evil dwells.

Let Light and Love and Power restore the Plan on Earth.

16. *Commentary on The Great Invocation*

The Great Invocation is a multi-layered tool which aligns the individual soul with the I AM Presence. Its three levels operate in the realms of Light, Love, and Will. It is a series of coded invocations. An explanation of each invocation follows:

From the point of Light within the mind of God
Let light stream forth into the minds of men.
Let light descend on Earth.

The Light of Truth opens the mind to its own God-self. The search for man's true nature usually begins with mental questioning, and this verse invokes Divine Truth to flood the mind, allowing us to realize that we are part of the Source, i.e., enlightenment. The "descent of light" results in each person's alignment with his or her Oversoul.

From the point of Love within the heart of God
Let Love stream forth into the hearts of men.
May Christ return to Earth.

This verse invokes the opening of the heart for compassion and understanding. The stream of Love into your heart results in alignment with the Christ Oversoul. "May Christ return to Earth" invokes the opening of each of us to the Unity Band, or Christ Consciousness.

From the center where the Will of God is known
Let the purpose guide the little wills of men —
The purpose which the Masters know and serve.

This verse opens you to being a Divine Servant. When your will is aligned with Divine Will, you become a Divine Instrument. Becoming a Divine Instrument is the "purpose which the Masters know and serve." "Masters" is not limited to Ascended Masters, but applies to each person as they come into their mastery. Coming into your mastery aligns you with your I AM Presence.

From the center which we call the race of men
Let the Plan of Love and Light work out
And may it seal the door where evil dwells.

"The Plan of Love and Light" refers to ascension. "Sealing the door where evil dwells" refers to the dissolution of the veil of separation. Only with a sense of separation can the illusion of evil be experienced. When each one of us has dissolved our veil of separation, the illusion will be banished and the Plan will work out.

Let Light and Love and Power restore the Plan on Earth.

A final invocation to Truth, Love, and Power in the ascension process.

About the Author ...

Tony Stubbs

Born in England in 1947, he states that he grew up like most ordinary boys in a big city. Tony received a scientific and engineering education, and holds a master's degree in Computer Science from London University. After moving to the United States in 1979, he continued in the computer field, but also "woke up" to metaphysics.

In 1988, he started to channel. Almost immediately, he made contact with Serapis (a higher aspect of his being) and began cooperative writing with Serapis. He maintains a close association with the members of the Angelic Outreach organization (which operates under the guidance of Tachi-ren and Archangel Ariel), with whom he shares a great deal of enthusiasm and accord.

Tony lives in Denver, Colorado. Up until now, he had spent much of his time running a technical computer institute and teaching computer classes at a local university. Like so many Lightworkers at this time, his life is currently undergoing major restructuring and Serapis has advised him to "Live without expectations." As this book goes to press, he is continuing to teach computer classes, but he is spending more time reading, meditating, and studying, while he waits for Spirit to show him what to do. As for forthcoming books, the old radio news line seems appropriate: "Stay tuned for further announcements ... !"

About the Publisher and Logo ...

The name "Oughten" was revealed to the publisher fourteen years ago, after three weeks of meditation and contemplation. The combined effect of the letters carries a vibratory signature, signifying humanity's ascension on a planetary level.

The logo represents a new world rising from its former condition. The planet ascends from the darker to the lighter. Our experience of a dark and mysterious universe becomes transmuted by our planet's rising consciousness — glorious and spiritual. The grace of God transmutes the dross of the past into gold, as we leave all behind and ascend into the millennium.

Publisher's Comment ...

Our mission and purpose is to publish ascension books and complementary material for all peoples and all children worldwide.

We currently serve over twenty authors who have books, manuscripts and numerous tapes in production. Our authors channel Sananda (Jesus), Ashtar, Archangel Michael, St. Germain, Archangel Ariel, Hilarion, Mother Mary, Kwan Yin, and other Ascended Masters. We are in the process of extending this information to all nations, through foreign translations. Oughten House Publications welcomes your support and association in this momentous and timely endeavor. We urge you to share this information with your friends and families, and to join our growing network of like-minded people. A reply card is included for your convenience. Blessings and peace be with you always.

Oughten House Publications

Our imprint includes books in a variety of fields and disciplines which emphasize the rising planetary consciousness. Literature which relates to the ascension process is our primary line. We are also cultivating a line of thoughtful and beautifully illustrated children's books, which deal with spirituality, angels, mystical realms, and God, the Creator. Our third line of books deals with societal matters, personal growth, poetry, and publications on extraterrestrials.

The list that follows is only a sample of our current offerings. To obtain a complete catalog, contact us at the address shown at the back of this book.

Ascension Books

The Crystal Stair: A Guide to the Ascension, by Eric Klein. — ISBN 1-880666-06-5, $12.95

An Ascension Handbook A practical, in-depth, how-to manual on the ascension process, by Tony Stubbs.
 — ISBN 1-880666-08-1, $11.95

Bridge Into Light: Your Connection to Spiritual Guidance A how-to book on meditating and channeling, by Pam and Fred Cameron. (A companion tape is also available.)
— ISBN 1-880666-07-3, $11.95

The Inner Door: *Channeled Discourses from the Ascended Masters on Self-Mastery and Ascension,* by Eric Klein.

   Volume One: ISBN 1-880666-03-0, $14.50
   Volume Two: ISBN 1-880666-16-2, $14.50

Earth's Birth Changes: St. Germain through Azena A shining new world is coming, channeled by Azena Ramanda. — ISBN 0-646-136-07-0, $19.95

Reality Maintenance 101 Create and maintain your "Christed Reality" by using these prayers and techniques, developed through Commander Augustavia Staresseenia. Item #1002B, $20.00

The Thymus Chakra Handbook A how-to booklet for understanding and using this wonderful chakra. Channeled from The Christ and Kwan Yin by Brenda Montgomery. Item 1004B, $8.50

On Eagle's Wings One of the books recommended in *The Crystal Stair*, this is a collection of communications "from the Universe," given to Ariana over several years. By Ariana Sheran and Friends. Item #1000B, $8.00

E.T. 101 Wit and wisdom to lighten your way on the path, recommended in *The Crystal Stair*. Co-created by Mission Control and Diana Luppi. — ISBN 0-9626958-0-7, $12.00

Lady From Atlantis Millenium after millenium, male rulers have repeatedly failed to bring peace to this planet. Now Ascended Lady Master Shar Dae returns to modern America, to pursue her goal of world peace and the ending of duality. By Robert V. Gerard — ISBN 1-880666-21-9, $11.95

Other Books for the Rising Planetary Consciousness

Intuition by Design Increase your "Intuition Quotient" through the use of this book and its accompanying set of 36 cards. A valuable tool for applying your intuitive intelligence to all aspects of the decision-making process in your life, by Victor R. Beasley, Ph.D. — ISBN 1-880666-22-7, $18.95

Synergic Power: Beyond Domination, Beyond Permissiveness This book examines the concept of power and how to use power *with* people, not over or against them. By James H. and Marguerite Craig. — ISBN 0-914158-28-7, $8.95

Children's Books

Nature Walk Introducing "Pelfius," the lively little Nature Spirit who lives among the trees, the rivers, and the stars. For children from 2 years and up (adults too!). A beautifully illustrated booklet, by Susan Hays Meredith.
— ISBN 1-880666-09-X, $5.95

Tapes: Discourses and Channeled Material

Ascension Tapes A series of channeled and meditation tapes on the ascension process, by Eric and Christine Klein. Request the list of available tapes from Oughten House.

Bridge Into Light Guides you through the exercises in the book, accompanied by original music composed by Fred Cameron. By Fred and Pam Cameron. Tape #2020T, $9.95

Parallel Realities Learn how to transcend linearity and access your multidimensional nature. By Tashira Tachi-ren. Tape Set #2003T, $44.00

Feminine Aspect of God Mother Mary tells us about her life and the role of women in Jesus' time. Channeled by Crea. Tape 2013T, $8.95

Extraterrestrial Vision, Vols. 1, 2, and 3 The history of the human race, the role of extraterrestrials in our history, how to tell positive ETs from negative ones, and what is coming in our future. The mid-causal entity Theodore, channeled by Gina Lake. Tapes #2010T, #2011T, and #2012T, $9.95 each.

Birthing the Era of God The music of Michael Hammer accompanies this guided meditation from The Divine Mother, spoken by Claire Heartsong. Tape #2017T, $13.00

Preparation for Ascension, #1 The I AM presence of Yeshua Sananda facilitates our ascension process with limitless love. Channeled by Claire Heartsong. Tape #2018T, $13.00

Other Tapes

Mary's Lullaby A healing meditation sent to us by Mary, Mother of Jesus. A soothing melody, combined with the angelic voice of Claire Applegate. A great meditation tape for toddlers, older children, and adults alike. Tape #5007T, $9.95

Song of Gothar A story of deep emotional healing, when the longings of the heart are given voice. By Deborah Nayanna Barrable. Appropriate for children and teenagers, as well as adults. Tape #5013T, $12.95

The Yogi from Muskogee, *Don't Squeeze the Shaman*, and *Enlightening Strikes Again* Famed entertainer Swami Beyondananda puts *fun*damental before *trance*ndental. A welcome break for comic relief on the spiritual path. Tapes #6002T, #6003T, and #6004T, $11.00 each.

Music Tapes

EL AN RA A beautiful piece of ascension music, to raise you to new levels of bliss. By Stefan Jedland. Tape #5017T, $11.95

Awakening Six lovely compositions embodying ascension energies through the voices of piano, strings, bells, and flutes. By Brad C. Rudé. Tape #5003T, $8.95

Tales from the Future One of the *Inner Landscapes* series by Michael Pollack, a best-seller defined as "music for the next generation after ascension." Tape #5014T, $10.99

Call of the Heart This special album of vocal and instrumental music arose from communing with God and nature. By Greg Gille. Tape #5006T, $10.95

Angels in the Rain Randall Leonard's original piano solos. Beautiful and relaxing music, recommended by Louise L. Hay. Tape #5000T, $10.00

Awake, Arise, Ascend Connie Stardancer's heartfelt singing, accompanied by Richard Shulman's exquisite musical arrangements. Tape #5012T, $10.00

A Higher Dimension Created near Mt. Shasta by Richard Shulman, these tranquil solo piano pieces inspire meditation, relaxation, and healing. Tape #5010T, $10.00

Products

Ascension Cards A collection of over 50 quotations and messages, selected from various books published by Oughten House. These cards may serve as a source of daily inspiration and to help one focus on one's own ascension process. They may also serve as a beautiful gift item for a friend or loved one. (Details in catalog)

Reader Networking and Mailing List

The ascension process presents itself as a new opportunity and reality for many of us on Planet Earth. Oughten House Publications now stands in the midst of many Starseeds and Lightworkers who seek to know more. Thousands of people worldwide are reaching out to find others of like mind and to network with them.

You have the opportunity to stay informed and be on our networking mailing list. Send us the enclosed Information Reply Card or a letter. We will do our best to keep you and your network of friends up to date with ascension-related literature, materials, author tours, workshops, and channelings.

If you have a network database or small mailing list you would like to share, please send it along.

Catalog Requests
&
Book Orders

Catalogs will gladly be sent upon request. Book orders must be prepaid: check, money order, international coupon, VISA, MasterCard, and Discover Card accepted. Include shipping and handling (US postal book rate): $3.50 first book; add 50¢ for each additional book. Send orders to:

OUGHTEN HOUSE PUBLICATIONS
P.O. Box 2008
Livermore • California • 94551-2008 • USA
Phone (510) 447-2332
Fax (510) 447-2376

Notes